WEBSTER: THE CRITICAL HERITAGE

THE CRITICAL HERITAGE SERIES

GENERAL EDITOR: B. C. SOUTHAM, M.A., B.LITT. (OXON.)
Formerly Department of English, Westfield College, University of London

For a list of books in the series see the back end paper

WEBSTER

THE CRITICAL HERITAGE

Edited by
DON D. MOORE
Professor of English, Louisiana State University

ROUTLEDGE & KEGAN PAUL
LONDON, BOSTON AND HENLEY

First published in 1981
by Routledge & Kegan Paul Ltd
39 Store Street,
London WC1E 7DD,
9 Park Street,
Boston, Mass., 02108, USA, and
Broadway House,
Newtown Road,
Henley-on-Thames,
Oxon RG9 1EN.
Printed in Great Britain by
The Thetford Press Ltd., Thetford, Norfolk
Compilation, introduction, notes, bibliography and index
Copyright © Don D. Moore 1981

Library of Congress Cataloging in Publication Data
Main entry under title:

Webster, the critical heritage.

(The Critical heritage series)
Bibliography: p.
Includes index.
1. Webster, John, 1580?-1625?—Criticism and
interpretation—Addresses, essays, lectures.
I. Moore, Don D.   II. Series.
PR3187.W4   822'.3   81-13838

ISBN 0-7100-0773-6   AACR2

22 JUL 1982

General Editor's Preface

The reception given to a writer by his contemporaries and near-contemporaries is evidence of considerable value to the student of literature. On one side we learn a great deal about the state of criticism at large and in particular about the development of critical attitudes towards a single writer; at the same time, through private comments in letters, journals or marginalia, we gain an insight upon the tastes and literary thought of individual readers of the period. Evidence of this kind helps us to understand the writer's historical situation, the nature of his immediate reading-public, and his response to these pressures.

The separate volumes in the *Critical Heritage Series* present a record of this early criticism. Clearly, for many of the highly productive and lengthily reviewed nineteenth- and twentieth-century writers, there exists an enormous body of material; and in these cases the volume editors have made a selection of the most important views, significant for their intrinsic critical worth or for their representative quality—perhaps even registering incomprehension!

For earlier writers, notably pre-eighteenth century, the materials are much scarcer and the historical period has been extended, sometimes far beyond the writer's lifetime, in order to show the inception and growth of critical views which were initially slow to appear.

In each volume the documents are headed by an Introduction, discussing the material assembled and relating the early stages of the author's reception to what we have come to identify as the critical tradition. The volumes will make available much material which would otherwise be difficult of access and it is hoped that the modern reader will be thereby helped towards an informed understanding of the ways in which literature has been read and judged.

B.C.S.

Contents

Contents

Introduction

In his address to the reader in the 1612 quarto of 'The
White Devil', John Webster, responding to charges of his
slowness as a writer, seems confident of his own critical
heritage:

> To those who report I was a long time in finishing this
> tragedy, I confess I do not write with a goose-quill,
> winged with two feathers, and if they will needs make
> it my fault, I must answer them with that of Euripides
> to Alcestides, a tragic writer: Alcestides objecting
> that Euripides had only in three days composed three
> verses, whereas himself had written three hundred:
> 'Thou tells't truth,' (quoth he) 'but here's the dif-
> ference, — thine shall only be read for three days,
> whereas mine shall continue three ages.'(1)

Indeed, as in his Preface to 'The Devil's Law Case',
Webster never seemed to doubt that his works would be
found worthy. And if 'The White Devil' failed at the Red
Bull Theatre, it was due to the absence of 'a full and
understanding auditory',(2) not to the absence of the
writer's art.
    More than three ages have now passed, and Webster's
self-evaluation has proven, in many ways, accurate. His
major tragedies, 'The White Devil' and 'The Duchess of
Malfi', are the focus of attention in the study, the
school, and, increasingly, on the stage. Dissertations
are written; symposia are held; editions are plentiful.
At the same time, however, Webster's prophetic comments
are not wholly accurate. For almost two ages Webster
was available, having not fully disappeared with his
fellows; but few seemed to care. And with his revival in the early nineteenth century, heralded by Lamb's
appreciation, Webster began to generate one of the most

peculiar critical histories of any author of any time:
by some he is praised unstintingly as being second only to
Shakespeare in tragic art, and he is damned to the lowest
circles by others. Since 1850 his tragedies have been
staged more often than those of any of Shakespeare's contemporaries except Jonson; the results have brought delight and dole in equal scale. Webster endures, but not
quite in the fashion he may have imagined: in 1949, for
example, we learned that Webster rose above his fellows
through his 'intellectual and spiritual insight',(3) but
elsewhere that there is, finally, 'something a trifle
ridiculous about Webster'.(4)

CONTEMPORARY REPUTATION

As has often been noted, what we know about Shakespeare
seems voluminous when compared with what we know of Webster
in his own time. Until recently, the primary biographical
facts were these: in 1602, Henslowe made five payments to
John Webster and several other playwrights; we have dates
for Webster's collaborative efforts; we know that 'The
White Devil' failed at the Red Bull Theatre in 1612 but
that 'The Duchess of Malfi' was produced at the Globe in
1614, representing a gain in prestige for the dramatist;
by 1615 Webster was a freeman of the Merchant Taylors'
Company; we have later dates of plays written alone and
with his fellows. However, Mary Edmond has recently discovered some valuable additions to these meagre facts,
concerning Webster's family:(5) through a study of wills
and other evidence she has made a probable case that the
dramatist's parents were John and Elizabeth Webster of
St Sepulchre's without Newgate, and that John senior and,
later, the dramatist's younger brother Edward were important figures in the rapidly developing road transport business as makers of waggons, carts, and coaches.(6) Records
indicate that the playwright's father had dealings with
theatre people and their pageantry in the early 1590s;
and given the last journeys taken by condemned men from
Newgate prison to their execution in one of Webster's
carts, we can agree with Edmond that 'it is not surprising
that his elder son's thoughts turned toward the stage, and
sombre themes'.(7) She further names, through wills of
two neighbours near Webster, a Sara Peniall as the dramatist's wife and his children as John, Elizabeth, Sara, and
others. Edmond conjecturally places Webster's birth in
1578 or not long after, and his death between 1632 and
1634.(8)

Yet we remain in a mist, to use a Websterian image, regarding his general reputation in his own time. Certain things are sure: from Webster himself we learn the fate of 'The White Devil' (No. 1), which was not surprising. The theatre audience at the Red Bull in Clerkenwell was 'a plain man's playhouse, where clownery, clamor, and spectacle vied with subject matter flattering to the vanity of tradesmen'.(9) Such a house might well have been confused by a drama of old conventions but troublingly new ideas, with characters who did not fit the older stereotypes. Webster did not lack confidence, however, and perhaps never did, as evidenced by his dedications to 'The Duchess of Malfi' (No. 2) and 'The Devil's Law Case' (No. 3). We have in the Preface to 'The White Devil' his well-known references to his colleagues; we note that he begins the list with the two serious and classical writers, Chapman and Jonson, and ends with the master writers of the popular theatre, Shakespeare, Dekker, and Heywood. There is little doubt that Webster would prefer to be read by the 'light' of the first two learned playwrights, and with Jonson's defensive Preface to 'Sejanus' before him, no doubt saw himself as above the popular theatre. Still, his 'good opinion of other men's labors' is not particularly effusive, and Webster here, as in the other dedicatory epistles, seems at this time an independent, confident man. That near the end of his career he would return in a collaborative role to the Red Bull was an unanticipated and probably an unpleasant irony: 'Keep the Widow Waking', written with Ford, Dekker, and Rowley, was performed there in 1624.

The commendatory verses for the 1623 edition of 'The Duchess of Malfi' (No. 4) are from three playwrights not praised in 'The White Devil' preface, and we may wonder at Webster's reputation in 1623 because of the absence of certain of those mentioned. Instead, we have Middleton, Ford, and Rowley, all collaborators with Webster but of different levels of learning and interests. Yet though Rowley's verse befits his usual hack level, Middleton's and Ford's do indicate a genuine awareness of the merit of the play; and we may note also that Middleton and Rowley wrote no other prefatory verse. The famous description by Henry Fitzjeffrey (No. 5) remains our only personal glimpse of Webster, and the unflattering portrait therein is the first of many intermittent but vivid assaults on Webster and his art which continue well into the twentieth century. Objecting to 'The Duchess' for religious reasons is Orazio Busino, Venetian envoy in England in 1618 (No. 6). That the play was thus available in 1618 indicates, along with the cast-lists, its theatrical success, as does the printing of 'The Duchess' in 1623 when presumably it was off the stage. Neverthe- less, after rising briefly to great heights, Webster's power in the field of tragedy declined: 'The Devil's Law Case' is a less than challenging play of episodic struc- ture belonging to 1616-20; there were dull collaborations; 'Appius and Virginia', in the 1620s (?), does manifest a unity of tone, but that tone is unexciting and simplistic. In his end was his beginning.

WEBSTER IN THE LATER SEVENTEENTH CENTURY

For a period of time afterwards we find Webster in the commonplace books (Edmund Pudsey had earlier garbled eight quotations from 'The White Devil', c. 1616) and as a ghostly influence on such writers as James Shirley, Nathaniel Richards, and Robert Baron. In 1648, an unlic- ensed royalist newsbook, 'Mercurius Pragmaticus', referred to 'famous Webster' in a roll-call of poets including Seneca, Sophocles, Shakespeare, and Jonson(10) (Webster being singled out for the lone adjective); but it is Samuel Sheppard who provides us with the one mid-century appreciation with his epigram on 'The White Devil' in 1651 and his inclusion of Webster in a literary hall of fame in his laboured epic 'The Fairy King' (No. 8). The latter effort includes Webster in a House of Eloquence, ranking behind More, Sidney, Spenser, Chapman, and Wotton. The work was never published, a blessing for the public. His epigram on 'The White Devil', however, marks the beginning of a rudimentary character criticism: Vittoria is a 'fam'd whore', Flamineo is 'The Devil's darling', and the like. Given the absence of any kind of real criticism, we have o settle for Sheppard. Webster shortly made his first of many appearances in poetic anthologies in John Cotgrave's 'The English Treasury of Wit and Language' (1655), and is represented by 104 quotations from his plays. We may credit Cotgrave as the first anthologist to present dra- matic poetry by minor as well as major dramatists, and to place the passages under topics from A to W, that is, from 'Accident' to 'World'. Webster ranks sixth behind Shakes- peare (154 quotations), Beaumont and Fletcher (112), Jonson (111), Chapman (111), and Greville (110).(11)
    The early 1660s found Webster on the stage once more: 'The White Devil' was performed twice in October of 1661 and again the following December; there would be another recorded performance in late summer of 1671. The quarto of 1671 tells us that it had been 'divers times Acted by the Queenes Maiestes seruants in Drury Lane'; the third

and fourth quartos (1665 and 1672) note performances at
the Theatre Royal by the King's Company. More successful
seems 'The Duchess of Malfi': it was performed on 30
September 1662, with London's finest talent. Betterton
played Bosola, Mary Saunderson was the Duchess, with Henry
Harris as Ferdinand. John Downes records that it was 'so
exceedingly excellently acted in all parts, chiefly Duke
Ferdinand and Bosola, it filled the house eight days suc-
cessively, proving one of the best stock tragedies'.(12)
Samuel Pepys, however, had some opinions of Webster which
sound similar to those of some modern reviewers (No. 9).
Taking advantage of this brief revival of Webster was
Francis Kirkman, who published 'A Cure for a Cuckold' in
1661 with a Preface which is of interest: 'As for this
play, I need not speak anything in its commendation, and
the author's names, Webster and Rowley, are (to knowing
men) sufficient to declare its worth.'(13) Again, Rowley
was in good company.
     Thus Webster was kept tenuously alive through sporadic
performances and new editions of his plays. 'Appius and
Virginia' was reprinted in 1654 (reissued in 1659) and
again in 1679, due to Betterton's adaptation called 'The
Roman Virgin'. (The actor's revision never saw print,
which may tell us something of its merit.) Webster's
appearance in play lists such as Edward Archer's (1656)
and Kirkman's (1661 and 1671) indicates that the reading
of old plays did not stop for a Civil War and a Restoration.(14) Edward Phillips made Webster the subject of a
brief but error-filled account in his effort at theatre
history in 'Theatrum Poetarum' (1675); William Winstanley
did little better in his 'Lives of the Most Famous English
Poets' (1687), usually copying indiscriminately from
Phillips. It remained for Gerard Langbaine to bring together the play lists and the attempt at biographies in
his 'Account of the English Dramatic Poets' in 1691 (No.
10), a revision of his 'New Catalogue of English Plays'
of 1688. His account is given here chiefly for the historical record; but for a century it was the standard
source for Webster documentation. In 1698 Charles Gildon
republished the material in his 'Lives of the Poets',
adding almost as an afterthought that Webster was at one
time clerk of St Andrew's parish, thus confusing the dramatist's biography for over a century. Dyce in his 1830
edition firmly challenged the accuracy of the remark,
C.W. Dilke having been dubious in his 'Old English Plays'
(1814-15) which included 'Appius and Virginia'.
     James Wright in 'Country Conversations' (1694) helps
bring the sparse Webster references to a placid and perhaps symbolic close at the end of the century. A country

gentleman, Trueman, chats with his visiting city friends
on a variety of topics, from the merits of the older drama
and the new to proper garden arrangement. We eventually
hear one Julio, upon seeing some picturesque ruins preserved by a neighbouring squire, quoting Antonio's 'ruins'
speech from 'The Duchess' (V, iii, 9-19). Indeed, we
learn that Julio was one 'who omitted no occasion to mag-
nify the wit of the dramatic poets of the last age'.(15)
The passage, soon to be the Webster favourite in eighteenth-
century anthologies, is ascribed to Webster, the play, and
the speaker, and is the only quotation in the book apart
from translated passages. Wright, son of Abraham Wright
(No. 7), produced in 1699 the 'Historica Histronica', in
which he briefly refers to 'The Duchess' as the first of
a group of plays that had the names of the actors set
against their parts.
  Between the publications of Wright, there had been a
touch of Webster in another play: Joseph Harris's 'The
City Bride' (1696) was a reworking of 'A Cure for a
Cuckold' with poetry turned to prose amid music, song,
and the latest in Restoration repartee. The plot at least
remained essentially Webster's. However, Webster was
briefly taken to task in 1698 for one aspect of his plot-
ting in 'The Duchess' (No. 11).
  Thus if the years immediately following the Restoration
were briefly propitious for Webster, the next twenty-five
years were not. He had not completely disappeared, but
we have fewer and fewer straws to grasp. Shakespeare,
Jonson, Beaumont and Fletcher remain visible, sometimes
on stage and in books of poetic miscellany, dedications of
Restoration plays, and in critical works of Dryden, Cowley,
and others.(16) Nevertheless, Webster, if less acknowledged,
still had an influence in the melodramas of Southerne, Otway,
and others who dealt with the themes of lust and betrayal.
As Allardyce Nicoll has noted,

  The horrible presentments that are put forward in so
  many of the Restoration tragedies, heroic and otherwise, make us realize that, if the poetic spirit of
  Webster and Ford was in many ways lost, certainly their
  love of blood and of riotous torment never was.(17)

THE EIGHTEENTH CENTURY

Generally speaking, there is no critical heritage of John
Webster between 1700 and 1800. The dramatic bibliographers
were acquainted with him; poetry anthologies sometimes
included him; and scholars, turning increasing attention

to the age of Shakespeare, knew his plays.(18)   But even
for Malone, Steevens, and Capell, Webster was for an age,
not for all time.   Pope's one allusion in 1728 sums up most
of the commentary: 'Webster, Marston, Goff, Kyd, and Massinger were the persons instanced as tolerable writers of tragedy in Ben Jonson's time.'(19)   And Webster's stage history
for over a century can be told as quickly: three performances of a revised 'Duchess of Malfi', and two adaptations,
one not staged, the other lasting two performances.

On 22 July 1707, 'The Unfortunate Duchess, or, The Unnatural Brothers' was performed at the lavish Queen's Hay-
market, the first playhouse to be constructed in the century.   Two more performances followed on 29 July and 8
August.   The reviser is unknown, but the cast was excellent,
including John Verbruggen, Mary Porter, John Mills, Barton
Booth, and others.   The text, in the form of the fourth
quarto, was published in 1708 and indicates cuts and stage
directions.   Missing was the pilgrim scene (III, iv), the
fables, and the lines in Act III, scene iii indicating a
son of the first marriage.   Some of the language is, of
course, purged: 'lecher' becomes 'lover', for instance,
amid other laundering.   Compared to what awaited Webster,
however, the 1708 text seems pure.

In 1707, Nahum Tate, plagiarist and poet laureate,
favoured his public with a newly published play called
'Injur'd Love, or, The Cruel Husband' (No. 12).   Nowhere
does Tate admit his theft (who would know?); he does admit
in an epilogue that he 'chose a Vessel that would bear the
shock / Of Censure; Yes, old built but Heart of Oak'.   The
vessel, however, cannot bear the shock of Tate.   Though 'The
White Devil' fares better than did 'King Lear' in Tate's
hands — some scenes follow in their regular Websterian
order with little rewriting, and the villains meet their
deaths as in the original — conformity and convention are
observed. Vittoria, no longer the blazing Jacobean femme
fatale, is truly innocent of adultery with Brachiano (making
the trial scene ridiculous), and, indeed, in her own praise
of Isabella's purity we realize we have reached the age of
sentimental drama, an age wherein, on stage at least, the
earth groans at the thought of a broken marriage.   It is
salutary to know that 'Injur'd Love' never injured an
audience: no record of a performance exists.(20)

On 18 December 1731, Lewis Theobald writes to William
Warburton:

I have apply'd my uneasie Summer Months upon the
Attempt of a Tragedy. *Sit verbo venia!* I have a
Design upon the Ladies Eyes, as the Passage to their
Pockets.... I'll indulge myself, in submitting a Pair
of soliloquies to you, as a taste of my poor Workman-

ship. I lay my scene in Italy. My heroine is a young
Widow Dutchess, who has two haughty Spanish Brothers,
yet enjoin her not to marry again. She, however, marries the Master of her Household on the morning I open
my scene....(21)

There follow two soliloquies from his 'tragedy' with lines
from Webster sometimes recognizable, but not apparently to
the scholar Warburton. Such was the state of Webster
scholarship.
    The play, now called 'The Fatal Secret' (No. 13), was
staged twice at Covent Garden on 4 and 6 April 1733, with
James Quin as Bosola, Lacy Ryan as Ferdinand, and Mrs Hallam as the Duchess; and it is worse than 'Injur'd Love'.
Theobald in his Preface, which affords us our one piece of
neo-classic comment on Webster, blames politics and the
weather for the brief run of the play; we can blame Theobald. Admitting his larceny in the Preface (one hopes he'd
been caught), he writes of Webster's violation of the
unities and his 'wild and undigested Genius'. In the process of taming and digesting this genius, however, Theobald
regularizes the play into an unintentional farce. If the
plot consequently moves more quickly, it is at the expense
of everything else. No children are born, obvious morals
are drawn, horrors are softened, Webster's lines disappear,
but in this brave new world the Duchess herself does not:
at the end of the play, having been safely stowed away by
Bosola, she emerges alive, well, and tedious. An anonymous
letter writer to the 'Grubstreet Journal' on 25 April, protesting the refusal of his own work by the theatre manager
who has instead staged lesser plays, reports triumphantly
that 'The Fatal Secret' 'met with the Fate it deserved'.(22)
On this note, Webster's plays left the English stages for
over a century.
    Indeed, it may be said that Webster left the English
consciousness for almost the same period, until Lamb's
'Specimens of the English Dramatic Poets' in 1808. There
are small sightings during the remainder of the century,
yet Webster is relegated even there to one of a crowd,
leading no individual life and noted only by anthologists
and scholars.
    In 1738 Thomas Hayward, drawing from the remarkable
library of Edward Harley, second Earl of Oxford, and with
the help of Harley's librarian, William Oldys, put together 'The British Muse' ('A Collection of Thoughts
Moral, Natural, and Sublime of our English Poets; who
flourished in the Sixteenth and Seventeenth Centuries').
Two hundred plays furnished proper comment on alphabetized
subjects (Cotgrave's legacy), from Adversity into the Y's.

If we pit Shakespeare against Webster in citations, the
score is 427 to 93, in Stratford's favour. The anthology
was published again in 1777 as 'Beauties of the English
Drama', and perhaps caught Lamb's attention. 'The White
Devil', not known even to Fielding when he parodied Tate's
'Injur'd Love' in 'The Tragedy of Tragedies, or the Life
and Death of Tom Thumb' (1731), reappeared for the reading
public when Robert Dodsley published his 'Old Plays' (1744).
Webster's play goes unannotated, but later editions in
1780 and 1825 include the erroneous 'parish clerk' biography (Gildon's causal contribution to the critical heritage in 1698) and list his plays and their dates. (The
1825 edition by Reed, Collier, and Gilchrist includes the
Fitzjeffrey portrait and Theobald's Preface to 'The Fatal
Secret', not much of an editorial favour.) Thus in 1744,
one could read 'The White Devil', but with Tate's 'King
Lear' playing at the Garden, one probably wouldn't bother.
    Webster is mentioned in David Erskine Baker's 'Bio-
graphica Dramatica' (1764) as a 'tolerable poet'; his
plays are listed with their earliest productions and with
fragmentary commentary: 'The Duchess of Malfi', for instance, 'is a story well known in history and was acted
with success'. Such was the process in the various 'histories' of the times.
    The scholars continued their work in Shakespeare, and
while we may patronize Lewis Theobald as artist, we owe
him a debt for his awareness that the method of editing
classical texts would also be of value in the editing of
the English classics.(23) Following Theobald's edition
in 1733, the regular procedure in the editing of Shakespeare came to include not only collation of texts and
explication of passages in an individual play with similar
speeches elsewhere in the canon, but also the comparison
of Shakespeare's work with that of his contemporaries.
Thus in 1783 Edward Capell's 'The School of Shakespeare',
the third volume in his 'Notes and Various Readings to
Shakespeare', included the 'Notitia Dramatica', a large
selection of extracts from old plays and from Shakespeare's sources. Capell includes from Webster the Preface
to 'The White Devil' and several somewhat garbled lines
from the play, the Induction to 'The Malcontent', three
quotations from 'Appius and Virginia', and a long dialogue from 'A Cure for a Cuckold'. Oddly enough, 'The
Duchess of Malfi' is overlooked, although 'The White Devil'
is on a list of plays that for Capell rival Shakespeare's.
Malone and Steevens also were busy reading old plays
(Malone would include a 'Historical Account of the English
Stage' in his 1790 edition of Shakespeare); yet in the
work of all three, the earlier dramatists were there pri-

marily to serve Shakespeare, to swell a progress and start
a scene or two.

Nevertheless, a historical approach was making its in-
roads. Thomas Warton had observed in 1754, 'In reading
the works of an author who lived in a remote age, it is
necessary that we should look back upon the customs and
manners which prevailed in his age, that we should place
ourselves in the writer's situation and circumstances.'
(24) Bishop Hurd insisted in his 'Defense of Romantic
Literature' (1762) that as Gothic and Grecian architecture
should be judged by the rules of form for each age, so
should types of poetry: 'Judge of 'The Faerie Queene' by
the classic models, and you are shocked with its disorder:
consider it with an eye to its Gothic original, and you
find it regular.'(25) Three years previously, Hurd had
had praise for the language of the age of Elizabeth: 'It
was pure, strong, and perspicacious, without affectation.
At the same time, the high figurative manner which fits a
language so peculiarly for the uses of the poet, had not
yet been controlled by the prosaic genius of philosophy
and logic.'(26)

Some of Hurd's observations were part of the growing
debate over the neo-classic concept of the unities, a
debate marked by increasing liberal criticism over the
cramping effect of observing the unities of time and place.
Daniel Webb in his 'Remarks on the Beauties of Poetry'
(1762) affords a typical observation:

> It is observable that the same critics who condemn so
> much in Shakespeare a neglect of the unities are
> equally forward in acknowledging the singular energy
> and beauty of his sentiments. Now it seems to me that
> the fault which they censure is the principal source
> of the beauties they admire. For as the Poet was not
> confined to an unity and simplicity of action he
> created incidents in proportion to the promptness and
> vivacity of his genius. Hence his sentiments spring
> from motives exquisitely fitted to produce them: to
> this they owe that original spirit, that commanding
> energy which overcome the improbabilities of the scene
> and transport the heart in defiance of the understand-
> ing.(27)

The argument would, in the following century, gain Webster
recognition by many for his own unity of design and tone;
but not in the eighteenth century. For a more popular
view, we have Oliver Goldsmith's comments in his 'Enquiry
into the Present State of Polite Learning in Europe' (1759).
Writing on revivals of Jonson, Massinger, and, above all,
Shakespeare, he complains that

Old pieces are revived, and scarcely any new ones are
admitted. The actor is ever in our eye, and the poet
seldom permitted to appear; and the public are again
obliged to ruminate over these hashes of absurdity....
Let the spectator who assists at any one of these newly
revived pieces specifically of Shakespeare only ask
himself whether he would approve of such a performance
by a modern poet? I fear he will find that much of
his applause proceeds merely from the sound of a name
and an empty veneration of antiquity.(28)

THE EARLIER NINETEENTH CENTURY

In a modestly brief autobiography written in 1827 at the
request of William Upcott, Charles Lamb added at the end
of an incomplete list of his works one comment: 'He was
also the first to draw the Public attention to the old
English Dramatists in a work called "Specimens of the
English Dramatic Writers who lived about the time of
Shakespeare", published about 15 years since.'(29) Lamb
was wrong only in the time lapse: it had been nineteen
years since his pioneering work in 1808 (No. 14). Otherwise, his remark is accurate.
    Lamb brought for the first time a genuinely critical
acumen to the works of the writers as opposed to the antiquarian appreciation of the anthologists and the historical
dictionaries. It was an impressionistic approach to the
plays as literature, not as antique curiosities, and owes
its method partly to the Longinian influence on Romantic
criticism, an emphasis on appreciative ecstasy in the
reader, rather than on an Augustan inquiry through ana-
lytic, judicial investigation. Bishop Hurd had earlier
written of the 'pure, strong, and perspicacious' language
of the age of Elizabeth; and Wordsworth only recently had
defined poetry as the 'spontaneous overflow of powerful
feelings' in his Preface (1802) to the 'Lyrical Ballads'.
As Wordsworth concentrated on 'fitting to metrical arrangement a selection of the real language used by men', so
Lamb, in printing large extracts from the dramatists,
chose scenes (rather than the anthologists' quotations)
of the 'deepest quality':

    The kind of extracts which I have sought after have been,
    not so much passages of wit and humour, though the old
    plays are rich in such, as scenes of passion, sometimes
    of the deepest quality, interesting situations, serious
    descriptions, that which is more nearly allied to poetry
    than to wit, and to tragic rather than to comic poetry.

The plays which I have made choice of have been, with
few exceptions, those which treat of human life and
manners, rather than masques, and Arcadian pastorals,
with their train of abstractions, unimpassioned deities,
passionate mortals, Claius, and Medorus, and Amintas,
and Amarillis. My leading design has been, to illustrate what may be called the moral sense of our ancestors. To show in what manner they felt, when they
placed themselves by the power of imagination in try-
ing situations, in the conflicts of duty and passion,
or the strife of contending duties; what sort of loves
and enmities theirs were; how their griefs were tem-
pered, and their full-swoln joys abated: how much of
Shakspeare shines in the great men his contemporaries,
and how far in his divine mind and manners he surpassed
them and all mankind.(30)

In 'the moral sense of our ancestors', 'the power of imagination', and other phrases we are reminded of Wordsworth's precepts and intentions, for in their own ways
both writers would restore a native poetic heritage. T.S.
Eliot would later criticize Lamb's poetic emphasis, and
hold him responsible for beginning a near-fatal dichotomy
between drama and poetry.(31) Indeed, all too often during the remainder of the century Webster is called a poet,
not a playwright. Nevertheless, Lamb's generous selections
and his marginalia led to renewed awareness of Webster and
his fellows, and to critical arguments over Lamb's observations well into our own time. And if Lamb on occasion
was overly enthusiastic, we can only regret that the earlier scholars and anthologists did not share the same fail-
ing.
    Something of a minor Elizabethan revival took place in
the journals in the years following the 'Specimens'. 'Blackwood's' in 1818 began a series on the early English drama
(No. 17) wherein Webster is found by John Wilson to be a
master of scenes rather than structure, although Wilson
accentuates the positive. Nevertheless, Wilson seems to
have been the first critic to consider the problem of losing the main character in the fourth act of a five-act play.
Other unsigned appreciations appeared in the 'European
Magazine' in October and November of 1820 and in the 'Retrospective Review' for 1823, neither of which bears reprinting.
The 'European Magazine' defends the early English dramatists
against Voltaire and neo-classic strictures: 'The spirit
of English tragedy is of too severe and mighty a character
to bend down to any rules but its own' (p. 302), although
the writer notes without real comment a great irregularity
in Websterian structure. The enthusiasm of the author in

the 'Retrospective Review' leads to the statement that
Webster is entitled 'to the gratitude of every lover of
the histrionic art; we say of the histrionic art because
they [his plays] are much better calculated for representation than most of our early dramas' (p. 88). We are
not told why this is so. Both writers quote appreciatively.
More important in reinstating the dramatist in the public mind were the lectures by William Hazlitt in 1819 (No.
19). Combining Lamb's evocative impressionism with more
specific historical and comparative criticism, Hazlitt is
the first to tell us that 'The White Devil' and 'The
Duchess of Malfi' 'come the nearest to Shakespear of any
thing we have upon record', a comparison both accepted
and challenged by critics of the future. Not surprisingly,
Hazlitt avoids real comment on Webster's structure, as
Hazlitt himself rarely attains a stylistic symmetry of
plan. Of interest is his preference for 'The White Devil',
since for Hazlitt the final horrors of 'The Duchess' 'exceed the just bounds' of tragedy. He notes that he writes
'under correction', a deferential bow, perhaps, to his
friend Lamb whose evocative tributes to the fifth act were
to become a standard point of argument.
     In 1830 came the text of Webster which would serve
readers for almost a century. Alexander Dyce, clergyman
editor, included in 'The Works of John Webster' the two
major tragedies, 'The Devil's Law Case', 'Appius and Virginia', 'Northward Ho', 'The Thracian Wonder', 'The
Famous History of Thomas Wyatt', and 'The Malcontent'.
His introduction (No. 23) remains of occasional merit.
Dyce testifies to Webster's 'overcharged' action in 'The
White Devil' which the imagination, nevertheless, 'receives as credible', and discusses Vittoria's role in the
trial scene with clear perception. He is among the first
to celebrate the wooing scene in 'The Duchess of Malfi',
'a subject most difficult to treat'; elsewhere his criticism is generally impressionistic appreciation. Dyce's
work received favourable notice: the London 'Literary
Gazette' commended 'Mr. Dyce's labours to the favour of
all literary persons' (17 April 1830, p. 255); Sir Walter
Scott, having included the two major tragedies in 'The
Ancient British Drama' (edited anonymously in 1810),
writes in 1831 to Dyce and notes Webster as 'one of the
best of our ancient dramatists'.(32) In an unsigned
article which commends Dyce in the 'Gentleman's Magazine'
(No. 25) we find a proto-Victorian reaction: Vittoria is
a threat to home and hearth, and the injured but faithful
wife Isabella moves the writer to tears. It is hardly a
full endorsement of Webster, who for the journalist had
sublime tragic power amid disjointed structure and unfortunate excesses.

1850-1900

On 20 November 1850, audiences at the Sadler's Wells
Theatre saw 'The Duchess of Malfi', the first staging in
over a century. With the production begins a new phase of
Webster's critical heritage, the responses to the plays as
acted. And this response is a divided one, to say the
least. Critics would disagree throughout the remainder of
the century, one side celebrating the poetic power of
Webster's tragic vision, while others, especially the
stage critics, would vigorously attack what they character-
ized as episodic structure, absurd improbabilities, and
gross excesses. And within the anti-Webster group would
come another complaint, that of decadence and immorality.
Nor surprisingly, the Victorian popular novelist and reformer Charles Kingsley first makes the charge not long
after the 1850 production. And while we may dismiss the
moral charges of the Victorians, the reviews of Webster on
the stage in the nineteenth century sound, on occasion,
sadly similar to those in our own time.(33)
     To be sure, what the Sadler's Wells audience saw was
not wholly Webster's 'Duchess of Malfi' but, as the printed
text informs us, one 'Re-Constructed for Stage Performance
by R.H. Horne'.(34) Richard Hengist (Henry) Horne, author
of the 'farthing epic' 'Orion' and well-known journalist,
editor, and critic, took Webster's play and turned it into
a stage piece that afforded certain actresses their most
famous role for the next twenty-five years in England and
the USA. However, in his adaptation, we lose a considerable portion of Webster. As Horne tells us in his introduction (No. 28),

All the terrors (shorn and abated of the excesses in
the original) are still left here in all their genuine
tragic force. But it must also be borne in mind that
nothing like a shocking *reality* must be presented; —
the whole being softened by stage arrangements — in
short, by *Art* — so as to be seen through a poetical
and refining medium.

This artistic softening results in a play of tight construction, fluent and unmemorable Fletcherian verse, and
a tone not of moral ambiguity but of melodrama, sentimental and black and white. Minor characters disappear,
and major characters constantly inform us as to their
intentions. Thus the Cardinal (now Cardinal Graziani)
confides in the audience often, manipulates Ferdinand,
and uses Julia, now sexually rehabilitated by Horne, as
an unwitting instrument in his melodramatic villainy. The

madmen are heard offstage in the tidying up of the plot:
those who hear them will assume the noise to be the ravings
of the mad Duchess, whose estate will then come into the
management of her brothers. (And, of course, 'shocking
reality' must be avoided.) The Duchess (now called Marina
and re-entering after her strangling to cry 'Mercy' and
die on stage) is not the occasionally sensual young woman
of Webster but one who shares this kind of business in the
torture scene with Bosola:

> *Bos.* Thou art an over-ripe fruit, that not being duly
> gathered, art fallen to rot on the soil. There's not a
> hand shall take thee up.
> *Duch. (Looking upwards.)* A hand *will* take me up! —
> A fallen fruit? No; I am a seed, whose mortal shell
> must lie and rot i' the earth before the flower can
> rise again to the light. *(Looking round as on her
> prison.)* Didst thou ever see a lark in a cage? —
> such is the soul in the body. The world is like its
> little turf of grass; and the heaven o'er our heads,
> like its looking-glass, only gives us a miserable know-
> ledge of the small compass of our prison.

We realize that something is dreadfully awry here: the
author has horned in and given to the Duchess Bosola's
original lines, thus completely reversing Webster's meaning. Yet George Henry Lewes (No. 28e), not an admirer of
Webster, felt that 'unless you have the two books side by
side, you cannot tell whether you are reading Webster or
Horne'. However, the 'Athenaeum' critic (No. 28c), having
read Webster better than Lewes but still objecting to having Webster exhumed, nevertheless realized that 'we have
here not even Webster'.
    But with sophisticated lighting (the stage slowly
darkened for moments of tension), scenic splendour (Horne's
text opens on 'A Bridge in Malfi with Gardens Beyond'), and
various sound effects (bells counterpointed the madmen's
cries), the Webster-Horne 'Duchess' played for twenty-five
years, though often to mixed reviews. There was even a
revision of the revision, published around 1860 in 'Cumber-
land's Acting Plays' by George Daniel (1789-1864), the mis-
cellaneous writer, satiric poet and friend of Lamb. While
not exactly on the level of Macready's stage restoration of
the Fool to 'King Lear', Daniel at least restored the dead
man's hand to 'The Duchess of Malfi'. And in the USA,
there were some remarkable last scenes, courtesy of 'Uncle
Tom's Cabin' (No. 30).
    While Isabella Glyn (No. 29), Alice Marriot, and Emma
Waller often received favourable personal notices (Glyn

built a career as the Duchess), the play did not always
receive the same. As noted earlier, a dichotomy came to
exist among Webster's critics. There would be those from
Swinburne through Eliot and into the later twentieth century who would attest to the power of Webster's tragic
vision, his revelation of man's inhumanity to man, his
stoicism in the face of horror and, throughout all, his
poetry. But the theatrical critics, particularly in the
new age of the 'well-made play', would decry the loose-
ness of Webster when seen on the stage, and in 'The Duchess'
the collection of corpses in the fifth act. Webster read
and Webster seen often generate different responses, even
with changes of taste and attitudes. In reviews from 1850
into the 1970s we realize that tears in the study sometimes
change to titters in the audience in many productions of
'The Duchess of Malfi', and the fault does not always seem
to be eccentric direction or acting. (To be sure, a 1919
production in which Ferdinand died standing on his head did
little to enhance Webster's poetic vision.)
     Thus William Poel's production of 'The Duchess' in 1892
(No. 41) which brought forth much of Webster's original
text (though amid cuts, rearrangement, and stylized horrors)
also brought forth William Archer, translater of Ibsen,
friend of Shaw, champion of a new, believable drama 'of
rational construction' (No. 42), and Webster's most voci-
ferous enemy. And though we may smile indulgently at
Archer, uninformed as he was about the Elizabethans, certain of his objections seem to be borne out by audience reactions to productions in our own time.(35)
     Attacking on the moral front were Canon Charles Kingsley
(No. 31) and, later, the traditionalist William Watson (No.
44), both of whom indirectly relate to Archer and his call
for real people acting rationally upon the stage, particularly if 'rationally' can be defined as 'morally'. Kingsley,
writing 'Plays and Puritans' not long after Horne's adaptation, protested the lack of moral purpose in the Elizabethans,
scoffing at the idea of improvement by negative illustration:

   As the staple interest of the comedies is dirt, so the
   staple interest in the tragedies is crime. Revenge,
   hatred, villainy, incest, and murder upon murder, are
   their constant themes and (with the exception of Shakespeare, Ben Jonson in his earlier plays, and perhaps
   Massinger) they handle these horrors with little or no
   moral purpose, save that of exciting or amusing the
   audience, and of displaying their own power of delineation in a way which makes one but too ready to believe
   the accusations of the Puritans.

Watson, over thirty years later, would complain in much
the same fashion:

> Cynicism, disgust, and despair were brief and casual
> refuges of Shakespeare's spirit. These moods are the
> permanent and congenial dwelling places of minds like
> Webster's.... The ethical infertility of such a pre-
> sentation of the world is manifest enough, but how short-
> sighted and shallow seems the criticism which professes
> to see any kinship between Shakespeare and a type of
> mind so defective in sanity of vision, so poor in humour,
> so remote from healthful nature, so out of touch with
> genial reality.

'Genial reality', however, is of course in the eye of
the beholder. For Swinburne (No. 36) in his long appreciation, far more enthusiastic than Lamb-like, for Symonds
(Nos 33, 39) and for other late Victorians, Webster's world
may have represented an escape from the reality Kingsley and
Watson represented. G.K. Hunter has suggested that

> The revival of interest in the early dramatists notice-
> able in the last quarter of the nineteenth century must
> be associated with the anti-Victorian or decadent strain
> in the library life of the time ... the exploration of
> past decadence is a liberation from the present and a
> means of justifying their own tastes.(36)

William Poel (No. 43) would defend Webster against Archer's
arrows by an appeal to the historical accuracy on Webster's
part, and his picture of the 'manners and morals of the
Italian Renaissance as they appeared to the imagination of
Englishmen'; and James Russell Lowell (No. 37) would do
something of the same. Although Poel meant Jacobean Englishmen, certain late Victorians found in Webster a corresponding attitude of mind, an attitude quite dissimilar to
Tennyson's seeming assurance of meeting his Pilot after
crossing the bar or Browning's cheery greeting to the un-
seen. Whether or not Webster was historically accurate is
unimportant, finally. Flamineo's 'at myself I will begin
and end' meant something more pessimistic yet more congenial to some readers than Henley's being master of his
fate. This fin de siècle attitude would be true for the
young Rupert Brooke in his vigorously written 'John Webster and the Elizabethan Drama', published posthumously in
1916. Brooke, more than any critic before him, could see
in Webster a unity of tone:

The end of the matter is that Webster was a great writer;
and the way in which one uses great writers is two-fold.
There is the exhilarating wav of reading their writing;
and there is the essence of the whole man, or of the
man's whole work, which you carry away and permanently
keep with you. This essence generally presents itself
more or less in the form of a view of the universe,
recognisable by its emotional rather than logical content.(37)

Yet some later Victorians could not go quite that far.
Gosse (No. 45), Ward (No. 35), Saintsbury (No. 38), even
Symonds, and others find Webster the master of mosaics, the
creator of the powerful dramatic moment. From Symonds's
introduction to Webster comes a remark which would, if
sometimes obliquely, be considered in many twentieth-century
studies:

in 'Vittoria Corombona' and 'The Duchess of Malfi', each
part is etched with equal effort after luminous effect
upon a murky background;   and the whole play is a mosaic
of these parts.   It lacks the breadth which comes from
concentration on a master-motive.

And Swinburne's observation that 'no poet is morally nobler'
indicates Webster's occupation in their minds: for the
Victorian lover of poetry, Webster's characters exist not
on a stage, but on a page.
    In 1899 came Sidney Lee's end-of-the-century estimate of
Webster for the 'Dictionary of National Biography' (No.
96) and it is unsatisfactory if unsurprising. Even though
the playwright is 'rarely coarse' and worked with a 'true
artistic sense', Webster 'with a persistence that seems
unjustifiable in a great artist ... concentrated his chief
energies on repulsive themes and characters'.   But before
the entry is over, we hear of the miraculous touches that
only Shakespeare could rival and the 'essential greatness
of his conceptions'.
    Chronicling varying responses in the critical heritage
of John Webster is somewhat reminiscent of the Duchess's
'going into a wilderness' / Where I shall find no path or
friendly clue / To be my guide'.   We can nevertheless sum-
marize generally that those who proclaim Webster's greatness emphasize throughout the century his power in creating
a dark and terrible poetic vision, a vision which for many
is a moral one.   Less wholehearted critics fall into three
broad categories.   First, there are those in the earlier
part of the century who emphasize the passion and Gothic
horror of Webster.   For many, Webster surpasses most in

the ability to create the terrible and the terrifying; yet
he flows with too great a facility and should be stopped
sooner. Fanciers of Webster's Gothic power exist, of
course, into the later nineteenth century. Second, there
are the critics among the later Victorians who see Webster
as the creator of the great poetic moment, yet without a
totality of meaning. The third group is dominated by
Archer, with support from the moralists, who care little
for personification but greatly for probability. Yet even
in this latter group of Webster's most implacable critics,
there is reluctant testimony to Webster's troublesome power.
Looking ahead to the twentieth century, further gene-
ralizations seem possible. The years would bring global
wars which would tragically attest to the credibility of
Webster's horrific vision of man's inhumanity. Writing on
the dead man's hand in 'The Duchess of Malfi', F.L. Lucas
in his great 1927 edition of Webster could note, 'Too
many of the present generation have stumbled about in the
darkness among month-old corpses on the battlefields of
France to be much impressed by the falsetto uproar which
this piece of "business" occasioned in nineteenth century
minds.'(38) And in 1945 a rare stage success of 'The
Duchess of Malfi' occurred in London shortly after com-
manders at Buchenwald and Dachau had proven the truth of
creations like Ferdinand and the Cardinal. In an accidental but telling stroke, the London 'Times' placed its
review of the play underneath five newly released pictures
of German concentration camps.(39)
    Webster's world is, alas, closer. Twentieth-century
critics have dealt with Webster with more sympathy and
with more enlightenment than were found in the nineteenth,
though in many ways they have built on what is recorded
here. And as in the previous century, there remains dis-
agreement still. Approaches have been made to a concept
of moral vision, with Irving Ribner and Robert Ornstein,
naming two of many, disagreeing over the degree attempted
or achieved.(40) Eliot's comment in 'Four Elizabethan
Dramatists' that Webster was a 'genius directed toward
chaos' (his view itself owing something to the later Victorians) generated differing responses from several Cambridge critics, among them Muriel Bradbrook and L.G.
Salingar. Though they conclude that Webster mixes convention with naturalism, Salingar is far more distressed
than Bradbrook.(41) Later critics such as Travis Bogard,
I.S. Ekeblad, and J.L. Calderwood turn to counterpoint and
ritual to explain Webster, finding a shaping vision based
on generic fusion of tragedy and satire (Bogard) or ritual-
istic images which bring a subtle order out of seeming
chaos.(42) J.R. Brown's excellent Revels introductions

to the tragedies draw on occasion from these approaches.
Most recently critics have moved away from questions of
moral vision and attempts to account for a unity of tone
and instead have considered the 'absurdist' element in
the plays, in which a 'conventional form' does not lead
to a 'conventional conclusion'.(43) Indeed, in a collection of essays on Webster in 1970(44) comparison is made
more frequently with the works of Beckett, Pinter, and
Ionesco than with any Jacobean dramatist, and for many
Webster has increasingly become our contemporary rather
than Shakespeare's.

But in the theatres Webster's fortunes continue to be
limited in spite of several major productions. After
efforts in the study in praise of Webster, critics in the
theatre have all too often continued to hear titters replacing terror and to see comedy replacing catharsis. The
fact remains that when we read metaphysical accounts of
how Flamineo's feigned death reflects subliminally the
appearance-reality motif and its reverberations throughout
'The White Devil', we should also remember that the scene
at the National Theatre in 1969 often provoked laughter.
Una Ellis-Fermor wrote many years ago that although 'The
Duchess of Malfi' was 'susceptible of a more or less
naturalistic presentation', its musical and poetic values
were 'utterly alien to any plausible stage representation'.
(45) In 1971 we had 'The Duchess' staged in two ways: at
the Royal Court in an avant-garde approach, and later at
Stratford in 'realistic' fashion. Reviews for both were
poor, with some critics rising to heights of humorous in-
vective. In a recent BBC television production, presented
naturalistically, Bosola seemed lost in a structural mist
and took longer to die than Bottom's Pyramus.

Sometimes it is obviously the director's fault; yet
sometimes it is Webster's. For all the appeal to myth,
ritual, symbol, and absurdist canons, Webster's plays on
stage admit to at least two confusing perspectives: the
court of Malfi, for instance, is seen in naturalistic
terms while Ferdinand and the Cardinal inhabit the nightmare world of the grotesque.(46) That a director can successfully fuse these perspectives in a truly satisfying
stage performance has yet to be fully demonstrated. It
is not surprising that we learn from the 1623 title-page
that the play was cut even from the time of its first performance. In the study the job of synthesis seems easier,
especially when we forget Ezra Pound's cogent remark that
'the medium of drama is not words, but people moving about
on a stage using words'. Nor was William Empson invoking
the shade of William Archer by claiming that it is 'clearly
wrong to talk as if coherence of character is not needed in

needed in poetic drama, only coherence of metaphor and so on'.(47)

A parallel which I drew some years ago still seems valid: Webster remains the Tennessee Williams of the Jacobeans. With women at the centre of his plays, Webster is, like Williams, darkly theatrical and poetically effective at his best, yet extravagantly rhetorical and implausible in his excesses. Like Williams, his outlook is intense but narrow, and inconsistent in tone even within that narrowness. And he, like Williams, has consequently generated a most divided critical heritage.

NOTES

1 'The White Devil', ed. J.R. Brown (1958), pp. 3-4.
2 Ibid., p. 2. Cf. Dekker's similar phrasing in 'If it be not Good, the Devil is in It' (1612).
3 David Cecil, 'Poets and Storytellers' (1949), p. 29.
4 Ian Jack, The Case of John Webster, 'Scrutiny', XVI (March 1949), p. 43.
5 Mary Edmond, In Search of John Webster, 'TLS', 24 December 1976, pp. 1621-22; see also her subsequent letters in 'TLS', 11 March 1977, p. 272, and 24 October 1980, p. 1201. Arriving too late for full consideration is M.C. Bradbrook's 'John Webster: Citizen and Dramatist' (1980), which builds on Edmond's discoveries and provides an in-depth picture of Webster's London.
6 The reference explains Fitzjeffrey's 'cartwright' (No. 5), usually taken to mean Webster's laborious workmanship, and makes more significant William Heminges' allusion in his mock elegy in 1632 to 'Webster's brother' who 'would not lend a coach' in order to provide a cortège for a missing finger, lost by a friend in a duel. R.G. Howarth had first noted the relationship between the references in 'TLS', 2 November 1933, p. 751. The 'Elegy on Randolph's Finger' is in the Bodleian Library, MS Ashmole 38, 26.
7 Edmond, op.cit., p. 1621.
8 Thomas Heywood in the 'Hierarchy of the Blessed Angels', licensed 7 November 1634, speaks of Webster in the past tense, telling us that the nickname of Fletcher and Webster 'was but Jack'. Heminges in 1632 refers to 'Webster's brother', seemingly a present tense. Thomas Hall thought he was alive in 1655 when he confused the dramatist with a popular preacher of the same name. Webster the vicar is attacked and called a 'Quondam Player' in Hall's 'Vindiciae Literarum'. Hall was confused, and the churchman no doubt surprised.

9 L.B. Wright, 'Middle Class Culture in Elizabethan England' (1935), p. 609.
10 Quoted in G.E. Bentley, 'Shakespeare and Jonson' (1945), p. 288.
11 See G.E. Bentley's John Cotgrave's 'English Treasury of Wit and Language' and the Elizabethan Drama, 'Studies in Philology', XL (April 1943), p. 192.
12 John Downes, 'Roscius Anglicanus', ed. Montague Summers (1928), p. 29. It would be staged again on 25 November 1668, 31 January 1672, and at court on 13 January 1686. ('The London Stage', ed. William Van Lennep (1965), I, p. 40).
13 Noted by F.L. Lucas, 'The Complete Works of John Webster' (1927), III, p. 29.
14 Tso-Liang Wang's 'The Literary Reputation of John Webster to 1830' (1975) studies the playlists effectively, pp. 1-38. Wang's book in the Salzburg monograph series has been a welcome aid for this entire period; I have also drawn freely upon my own 'John Webster and His Critics, 1617-1964' (1966) and referred to G.K. and S.K. Hunter's 'John Webster: A Critical Anthology' (1969).
15 James Wright, 'Country Conversations', ed. Charles Whibley (1927), p. 57.
16 Cf. Herbert Weisinger, The Seventeenth Century Reputation of the Elizabethans, 'Modern Language Quarterly', VI (March 1945), pp. 13-21.
17 Allardyce Nicoll, 'History of Restoration Drama 1660-1700' (1928), p. 120.
18 Cf. R.D. Williams, Antiquarian Interest in the Elizabethan Drama Before Lamb, 'PMLA', LIII (June 1938), pp. 434-44.
19 Quoted by Joseph Spence, 'Anecdotes, Observations, and Characters of Books and Men', ed. S.W. Singer, newly introduced by Barnaby Dobree (1964), p. 44.
20 Wang, op.cit., studies Tate's burglary as does Hazleton Spencer, Nahum Tate and 'The White Devil', 'Journal of English Literary History', I (1934), pp. 235-49.
21 Quoted in R.F. Jones, 'Lewis Theobald' (1919), p. 291.
22 Reprinted in the 'Gentleman's Magazine' (1733), p. 194. Wang, op.cit., also considers Theobald's version, as does R.K. Kaul in What Theobald Did to Webster, 'Indian Journal of English Studies', II (1961), pp. 138-44.
23 Cf. Earl Wasserman, The Scholarly Origin of the Elizabethan Revival, 'Journal of English Literary History', IV (September 1937), pp. 213-44.
24 Thomas Warton, Observations on The Fairy Queen, 'Eighteenth Century Essays', ed. Scott Elledge (1961), II, 772. Pope, of course, had in 1725 made his famous re-

mark about the futility of judging Shakespeare by Aris-
totle's rules; Johnson in 1765 would say that the
unities might be sacrificed successfully to variety.
25 Richard Hurd, 'Taste and Criticism in the Eighteenth
   Century', ed. H.A. Needham (1952), p. 146.
26 Richard Hurd, 'Letters on Chivalry and Romance', ed.
   Edith Morley (1911), pp. 71-2.
27 'Shakespeare: The Critical Heritage', ed. Brian Vickers,
   IV (1976), p. 519.
28 'Works of Oliver Goldsmith', ed. Peter Cunningham (1854),
   II, pp. 67-8. The strict Licensing Act of 1736 no doubt
   discouraged some potential playwrights.
29 Quoted by E.V. Lucas in 'The Works of Charles and Mary
   Lamb' (1904), IV, p. 597.
30 Ibid., p. 1. Lamb's selections were later often cited
   by others in the journals. Stendhal, in a chapter of
   'Armance' (1827), quotes part of Cornelia's dirge as an
   epigraph.
31 Cf. T.S. Eliot, The Possibility of a Poetic Drama in
   'The Sacred Wood' (1928) and Four Elizabethan Dramatists
   in 'Elizabethan Essays' (1934). Eliot himself would review 'The Duchess of Malfi' in 'Arts and Letters', III
   (Winter 1920), pp. 36-9. The production was a disaster,
   and Eliot's commentary is little better, with its
   several surprisingly untenable remarks on the staging
   of poetic drama. Eliot also did a radio critique of
   Webster, reprinted in the 'Listener', 18 December 1941,
   pp. 825-6. See my discussion of Eliot's influential
   role in Webster criticism in 'Webster and His Critics',
   pp. 97-108.
32 'Letters of Sir Walter Scott', ed. H.J.C. Grierson (1937),
   XII, 1. Making Webster further available for the Victorians would be W.C. Hazlitt's four-volume edition of
   Webster in 1857, reprinted in 1897. Generally an inferior copy of Dyce.
33 From reviews of 'The Duchess of Malfi' in November 1892
   and July 1971: 'At moments when the audience should have
   wept, it tittered' ('Nation'); 'Bosola confesses to
   having some conscience and kills his fellow villains.
   And the audience titters and goes home' ('Spectator').
   I do not mean to imply that all Webster productions
   meet with titters and failure, but the record is not a
   happy one.
34 Published by John Tallis in 1850. Two other texts exist,
   the Lord Chamberlain's licensing copy (BM Add. MS 43031,
   vol. CLXVII) and Samuel Phelps's prompt-book in the
   Folger Library (Cat. No. D. b. 5-9). A careful study of
   Horne's revision is in Frank Wadsworth's Shorn and
   Abated: British Performances of 'The Duchess of Malfi',

'Theatre Survey', X (1969), pp. 89-104.

35 Eliot in Four Elizabethan Dramatists, op. cit., commented on a paradoxical similarity between Archer and Swinburne in that both are discussing the distinction between poetry and drama: 'Swinburne as well as Mr. Archer allows us to entertain the belief that the difference between modern drama and Elizabethan drama is represented by a gain of dramatic technique and the loss of poetry.' In this essay, however, originally written in 1924, we end with an inverted similarity between Archer and Eliot: the weakness of the Elizabethans is not their lack of realism 'but it is the same weakness of modern drama, it is the lack of a convention'.

36 G.K. Hunter, op.cit., p. 53.

37 Rupert Brooke, 'John Webster and the Elizabethan Drama' (1916), p. 161.

38 F.L. Lucas, op. cit., I, pp. 33-4.

39 As I first noted in 'John Webster and His Critics', p. 155. See also Edmund Wilson's observations in Notes at the End of a War, published originally in the 'New Yorker', 2 June 1945, p. 47.

40 Cf. Irving Ribner's 'Jacobean Tragedy: The Quest for Moral Order' (1962) and Robert Ornstein's 'The Moral Vision of Jacobean Tragedy' (1960).

41 Cf. Muriel Bradbrook's 'Themes and Conventions of Elizabethan Tragedy' (1935) and L.G. Salingar's Tourneur and the Tragedy of Revenge in 'The Age of Shakespeare', ed. Boris Ford (1956). Salingar's is an updating of a 'Scrutiny' article in 1938. In her recent 'John Webster' (see. n. 5 above) Bradbrook relates Webster's effort to embody incompatibles to his 'difficult position between the gentry and the citizens. Webster constantly recalls, delicately and indirectly, the struggle of such a divided self.' She suggests that Webster was also influenced by the baroque art of Inigo Jones, 'the movement and perspective of his masques', thus disagreeing in effect with Ralph Berry (see n. 43 below).

42 Cf. Travis Bogard's 'The Tragic Satire of John Webster' (1955), I.S. Ekeblad's The 'Impure Art' of John Webster, 'Review of English Studies', IX (August 1958), pp. 253-67, and J.L. Calderwood's The Duchess of Malfi: Styles of Ceremony, 'Essays in Criticism', XII (1962), pp. 133-47.

43 Norman Rabkin (ed.), 'Twentieth Century Interpretations of "The Duchess of Malfi"', p. 8. Ralph Berry, in 'The Art of John Webster' (1972), sees in the dramatist's technique the principles of early baroque artistry, and

further claims for many of Webster's characters an exis-
tential outlook of which Camus would approve. And we
may hope that Maurice Charney has helped terminate
Webster-Shakespeare comparisons with his Webster vs.
Middleton, or the Shakespearean Yardstick in Jacobean
Tragedy in 'English Renaissance Drama', ed. Standish
Henning, Robert Kimbrough, and Richard Knowles (1976).
Charney sensibly suggests that we centre on what is dis-
tinctive and un-Shakespearean in the Jacobean dramatists.
44 'John Webster', ed. Brian Morris (1970), Mermaid Critical
Commentaries.
45 Una Ellis-Fermor, 'The Jacobean Drama' (1936), pp. 43-4.
46 Cf. Lois Potter's Realism versus Nightmare: Problems of
Staging 'The Duchess of Malfi', 'The Triple Bond', ed.
Joseph Price (1975), pp. 170-89. It is reassuring to
note some positive reviews for a staging of 'The Duchess'
at the Round House, London, in April 1981. For the
'Guardian', Adrian Noble's production preserved 'the
Websterian balance between decadence and tenderness'
(12 April 1981, p. 25).
47 William Empson, 'The Structure of Complex Words' (1951),
p. 231.

Comments

1. WEBSTER ON 'THE WHITE DEVIL'

1612

In something of a Declaration of Independence from the
popular theatre, Webster in his Preface to 'The White
Devil' defends his play after its failure at the Red Bull
Theatre (see Introduction). From J.R. Brown's Revels edition of 'The White Devil' (1958), pp. 2-4.

TO THE READER

In publishing this tragedy, I do but challenge to myself
that liberty, which other men have ta'en before me; not
that I affect praise by it, for, *nos haec novimus esse
nihil*,(1) only since it was acted, in so dull a time of
winter, presented in so open and black a theatre, that it
wanted (that which is the only grace and setting out of a
tragedy) a full and understanding auditory: and that
since that time I have noted, most of the people that come
to that playhouse, resemble those ignorant asses (who
visiting stationers' shops their use is not to inquire for
good books, but new books) I present it to the general
view with this confidence:

> *Nec rhoncos metues, maligniorum,*
> *Nec scombris tunicas, dabis molestas.*(2)

If it be objected this is no true dramatic poem,(3) I
shall easily confess it, — *non potes in nugas dicere*

plura meas: ipse ego quam dixi,(4) — willingly, and not ignorantly, in this kind have I faulted: for should a man
present to such an auditory, the most sententious tragedy
that ever was written, observing all the critical laws, as
height of style, and gravity of person, enrich it with the
sententious *Chorus*, and as it were lif 'n death, in the passionate and weighty *Nuntius*: yet after all this divine
rapture, *O dura messorum ilia*,(5) the breath that comes
from the uncapable multitude is able to poison it, and ere
it be acted, let the author resolve to fix to every scene,
this of Horace,

———*Haec hodie porcis comedenda relinques.*(6)

To those who report I was a long time in finishing this
tragedy, I confess I do not write with a goose-quill,
winged with two feathers, and if they will needs make it
my fault, I must answer them that of Euripides to Alcestides, a tragic writer: Alcestides objecting that Euripides had only in three days composed three verses,
whereas himself had written three hundred: 'Thou tell'st
truth,' (quoth he) 'but here's the difference, — thine
shall only be read for three days, whereas mine shall
continue three ages.'
   Detraction is the sworn friend to ignorance: for mine
own part, I have ever truly cherish'd my good opinion of
other men's worthy labours, especially of that full and
height'ned style of Master Chapman, the labour'd and
understanding works of Master Jonson: the no less worthy
composures of the both worthily excellent Master Beaumont,
and Master Fletcher: and lastly (without wrong last to be
named) the right happy and copious industry of Master
Shakespeare, Master Dekker, and Master Heywood, wishing
what I write may be read by their light: protesting, that,
in the strength of mine own judgement, I know them so
worthy, that though I rest silent in my own work, yet to
most of theirs I dare (without flattery) fix that of Martial:

———*non rorunt, haec monumenta mori.*(7)

Notes

1 'We know these things are nothing' (Martial, XIII, 2).
2 'You [the poet's book] will not fear the sneers of the
  malicious, nor be used for wrapping mackerel' (Martial,
  IV, 86).
3 Cf. Jonson's earlier and similar defence in his Preface
  to 'Sejanus' (1605).
4 'You cannot say more against my trifles than I have said

myself' (Martial, XIII, 2).
5 'O strong stomachs of harvesters' (Horace, 'Epodes', III,
   4; an allusion to their love of garlic).
6 'What you leave will be for the pigs to eat today'
   (Horace, 'Epistles', I, vii, 19).
7 'These monuments do not know how to die' (Martial, X, ii,
   12); comparing literature with ruined tombs).

2. WEBSTER'S VIEW OF 'THE DUCHESS OF MALFI'

1623

From Webster's dedication of his play, first staged c.
1614 by the King's Men to a response happily unlike that to
'The White Devil'. The play is dedicated to George Harding,
Baron Berkeley, who also received Burton's dedication of
the 'Anatomy of Melancholy' (1621). In J.R. Brown's Revels
edition (1964), p. 3.

I am confident this work is not unworthy your Honour's
perusal for by such poems as this, poets have kissed the
hands of great princes, and drawn their gentle eyes to
look down upon their sheets of paper, when the poets themselves were bound up in their winding sheets. The like
courtesy from your Lordship, shall make you live in your
grave, and laurel spring out of it; when the ignorant
scorners of the Muses (that like worms in libraries seem
to live only to destroy learning) shall wither, neglected
and forgotten. This work and myself I humbly present to
your approved censure, it being the utmost of my wishes,
to have your honourable self my weighty and perspicuous
comment: which grace so done me, shall ever be acknowledged.
     By your Lordship's in all duty and observance,
                                            John Webster

3. THE DEDICATION OF 'THE DEVIL'S LAW CASE'

1623

Webster again is certain that the greatest of Caesars have
happily approved lesser works than 'The Devil's Law Case',
which was probably staged c. 1617-20. The play is dedicated to Sir Thomas Finch, grandson of Thomas Heneage, vice-
chamberlain in the Queen's household. In 'The Complete
Works of John Webster', ed. F.L. Lucas (1927), II, p. 235.

Sir, let it not appear strange that I do aspire to your
patronage. Things that taste of any goodness love to be
sheltered near goodness. Nor do I flatter in this, which
I hate; only touch at the original copy of your virtues.
Some of my other works, as 'The White Devil', 'The Duchess
of Malfi', 'Guise'(1) and others, you have formerly seen.
I present this humbly to kiss your hands and to find your
allowance. Nor do I much doubt it, knowing the greatest
of the Caesars have cheerfully entertained less poems than
this; And had I thought it unworthy I had not enquired
after so worthy a patronage. Yourself I understand to be
all courtesy. I doubt not therefore of your acceptance,
but resolve that my election is happy. For which favour
done me I shall ever rest
                        Your Worship's humbly devoted
                                            John Webster

Note

1 Although Webster's 'The Guise' is mentioned in Archer's
  playlist in 1656, it has since disappeared. It possibly
  followed 'The Duchess of Malfi' in Webster's career, and
  is a major loss in the Webster canon.

4. THREE POEMS FOR 'THE DUCHESS'

1623

Thomas Middleton, William Rowley, and John Ford wrote the commendatory verses for the 1623 quarto of 'The Duchess of Malfi'. Middleton had collaborated with Webster many years earlier; Rowley and Ford would do so shortly. Interestingly, none of the three is mentioned in Webster's salute to his colleagues in the Preface to 'The White Devil' (see Introduction). From Brown's edition of 'The Duchess of Malfi' (1958), pp. 4-5.

In the just worth of that well-deserver, Mr. John Webster, and upon this masterpiece of tragedy.

In this thou imitat'st one rich, and wise,
That sees his good deeds done before he dies;
As he by works, thou by this work of fame,
Hast well provided for thy living name.
To trust to others' honourings is worth's crime—
Thy monument is rais'd in thy life-time;
And 'tis most just; for every worthy man
Is his own marble, and his merit can
Cut him to any figure and express
More art than Death's cathedral palaces,
Where royal ashes keep their court. Thy note
Be ever plainness, 'tis the richest coat:
Thy epitaph only the title be—
Write, 'Duchess', that will fetch a tear for thee,
For who e'er saw this duchess live, and die,
That could get off under a bleeding eye?

In Tragaediam.

Ut lux ex tenebris ictu percussa Tonantis,
Illa, ruina malis, claris fit vita poetis.(1)
                              Thomas Middletonus,
                              Poeta & Chron. Londinensis.

To his friend, Mr. John Webster, upon his 'Duchess of Malfi'.

I never saw thy duchess till the day
That she was lively body'd in thy play;

Howe'er she answer'd her low-rated love,
Her brothers' anger did so fatal prove,
Yet my opinion is, she might speak more,
But never, in her life, so well before.

                                              Wil. Rowley.

To the reader of the author, and his 'Duchess of Malfi'.

Crown him a poet, whom nor Rome, nor Greece,
Transcend in all theirs, for a masterpiece:
In which, whiles words and matter change, and men
Act one another, he, from whose clear pen
They all took life, to memory hath lent
A lasting fame, to raise his monument.

                                              John Ford.

Note

1 'To Tragedy: As light from darkness springs at the
  thunderer's stroke, / So she brings ruin to the wicked
  and life to the poet.' Middleton had been appointed
  City Chronologer in 1620.

5. FITZJEFFREY'S PORTRAIT OF WEBSTER

1617

The one contemporary picture of Webster is furnished by
Henry Fitzjeffrey of Lincoln's Inn in a satirical poem
called Notes from Blackfriars, printed in 'Certain Elegies
by Sundry Excellent Wits', although the chief wit seems to
have been Fitzjeffrey. The author describes, one by one,
types in an audience at Blackfriars, and it is possible
that Webster, after his successful if temporary emancipa-
tion from the Red Bull, may have become a noticeable figure
in the world of the Blackfriars Theatre. Thus Fitzjeffrey,
as Robert Greene in 1592, may be reacting to another 'up-
start crow' with pretensions to serious drama and criticism. We may note the imputation of slowness in writing,
the same charge which had provoked Webster's response in
the Preface to 'The White Devil' five years previously.
The 'cartwright' term, given recent discoveries, surely

alludes to the business of Webster's father and brother.
The Fitzjeffrey account is quoted by Lucas, 'Works', I,
p. 55.

But hist! with him, crabbed Websterio,
The playwright-cartwright (whether either!). Ho!
No further. Look as you'd be looked into;
Sit as ye would be read. Lord! who would know him?
Was ever man so mangled with a poem?
See how he draws his mouth awry of late,
How he scrubs, wrings his wrists, scratches his pate.
A midwife, help! By his brain's coitus
Some centaur strange, some huge Bucephalus,
Or Pallas, sure, engendered in his brain,
Strike Vulcan, with thy hammer once again.
This is the critic that of all the rest
I'd not have view me, yet I fear him least.
Here's not a word cursively I have writ
But he'll industriously examine it,
And in some twelve months hence, or thereabout,
Set in a shameful sheet my errors out.
But what care I? It will be so obscure
That none shall understand him I am sure.(1)

Note

1 For Webster's differences with the lawyers at Lincoln's
Inn, see M.C. Bradbrook's 'John Webster' (1980), pp.
167-9.

6. AN ITALIAN ENVOY COMMENTS ON 'THE DUCHESS'

1618

Orazio Busino, a Venetian envoy in England, describes 'on
another occasion' what seems to be Act III, scene iv of
'The Duchess of Malfi' and, assuming Busino could not distinguish Julia from the Duchess, the death of Julia in V,
ii. It is a confused account and may be based on hearsay.
Nevertheless, the account suggests a revival in 1618. From

Busino's 'Anglopotrida', a manuscript in the Marciana
library in Venice and noted by E.E. Stoll in his 'John
Webster' (1905), p. 29.

The English scoff at our religion as disgusting and merely
superstitious; they never put on any public show whatever,
be it tragedy or satire or comedy, into which they do not
insert some Catholic churchman's vices and wickednesses,
making mock and scorn of him, according to their taste,
but to the dismay of good men. In fact, a Franciscan friar
was seen by some of our countrymen introduced into a comedy
as a wily character chock-full of different impieties, as
given over to avarice as to lust. And the whole thing
turned out to be a tragedy, for he had his head cut off on
open stage. On another occasion they showed a cardinal in
all his grandeur, in the formal robes appropriate to his
station, splendid and rich, with his train in attendance,
having an altar erected on the stage, where he pretended to
make a prayer, organizing a procession; and then they
produced him in public with a harlot on his knee. They
showed him giving poison to one of his sisters, in a question of honour. Moreover he goes to war, first laying
down his cardinal's habit on the altar, with the help of
his chaplains, with great ceremoniousness; finally he has
his sword bound on and dons the soldier's sash with so much
panache you could not imagine it better done. And all this
was acted in condemnation of the grandeur of the Church,
which they despise and which in this kingdom they hate to
the death.

From London
7 February 1618

7. ABRAHAM WRIGHT'S COMMONPLACE BOOK

c. 1650

From 'Excerpta Quaedam per A.W. Adolescentem' (BM Add. MS
22068). Wright (1611-90), royalist clergyman and collector
of play manuscripts, used a commonplace book as one means
of instruction for his son James (1643-1713), later a
theatre historian. Wright records and comments on excerpts
from several dramatists, and his observations on Webster

illustrate his awareness of the varied approaches by which
a play may be judged. J.G. McManaway studies the MS in
'Studies in Honor of De Witt T. Starnes' (1967).

'The Duchess of Malfi'

A good play, especially for the plot at the latter end,
otherwise plain. In his language he uses a little too
much of scripture as in the first Act, speaking of a captain full of wounds, he says he [was] like the children
of Ishmael [all in tents]. And which is against the laws
of the scene, the business was two years a-doing, as may
be perceived by the beginning of the third Act where
Antonio has three children by the Duchess, when in the
first Act he had but one [sic].

'The White Devil'

But an indifferent play to read, but for the presentments
I believe good. The lines are too much rhyming. [Wright
praises the scene of the murder of the Duke.]

'The Devil's Law Case'

But an indifferent play. The plot is intricate enough,
but if rightly scanned will be found faulty by reason many
passages do either not hang together, or if they do it is
so sillily that no man can perceive them likely to be ever
done.

8. SINGULAR PRAISE FROM SAMUEL SHEPPARD

1651

The solitary mid-century appreciation comes from Samuel
Sheppard (c. 1624-55), royalist poet, satirist, and journalist. His epigram of 'The White Devil' serves mainly to
prove that Webster had not disappeared and marks an early
effort at rudimentary character sketches. 'The Fairy
King' (1648-54), an unpublished manuscript in the Bodleian,

includes a House of Eloquence wherein Webster has, oddly
for the time, a better place than Jonson. The third of the
'noble tragedies' may be the lost 'Guise'; or it may be
the tragi-comedy 'The Devil's Law Case'. From (a) 'Epigrams
Theological, Philosophical, and Romantic' (1651), p. 133;
and (b) 'The Fairy King', quoted in Hyder E. Rollins,
Samuel Sheppard and his Praise of Poets, 'Studies in
Philology', XXIV (April 1927), p.554.

(a) On Mr. Webster's Most Excellent Tragedy Called 'The
White Devil'

> We will no more admire Euripides,
> Nor praise the tragic strains of Sophocles;
> For why? Thou in this tragedy has framed
> All real worth that can in them be named.
> How lively are thy persons fitted, and
> How pretty are thy lines! Thy verses stand
> Like unto precious jewels set in gold
> And grace thy fluent prose. I once was told
> By one well skilled in Arts he thought thy play
> Was only worthy fame to bear away
> From all before it. Brachiano's ill—
> Murdering his Duchess hath by thy rare skill
> Made him renowned, Flamineo such another—
> The Devil's darling, murderer of his brother.
> His part — most strange! — given him to act by thee
> Doth gain him credit and not calumny.
> Vittorio Corombona, that famed whore,
> Desperate Lodovico weltering in his gore,
> Subtle Francisco — all of them shall be
> Gazed at as comets by posterity.
> And thou meantime with never-withering bays
> Shall crowned be by all that read thy lays.

(b) 'The Fairy King'

> Webster the next, though not so much of note
> Nor's name attended with such noise and crowd,
> Yet by the Nine and by Apollo's vote,
> Whose groves of bay are for his head allowed—
> Most sacred spirit (some may say I dote),
> Of thy three noble tragedies be as proud
> As great voluminous Jonson; thou shalt be
> Read longer and with more applause than he.

9. SAMUEL PEPYS ON WEBSTER

1661, 1662, 1666, 1668, 1669

Extracts from the 'Diary', ed. H.B. Wheatley (1893-9).
Pepys proves happily inconsistent in his reactions to Web-
ster. The 1662 production with Betterton had some success
(see Introduction); 'Ianthe' was Mary Saunderson, later
Mrs Betterton. 'The Roman Virgin' was an adaptation of
'Appius and Virginia' by Betterton in 1669.

---

2 October 1661: ...we went to the Theatre, but coming late
and sitting in an ill place I never had so little pleasure
in a play in my life; yet it was the first time that ever
I saw it — 'Victoria Corombona'. Methinks a very poor
play. (ii, 114)

4 October 1661: Then Captain Ferrers and I to the Theatre,
and there came too late; so we stayed and saw a bit of
'Victoria' which pleased me worse than it did the other
day. So we stayed not to see it out, and drank a bottle
or two of China ale. (ii, 116)

30 September 1662: ...after dinner we took coach and to the
Duke's playhouse, where we saw 'The Duchess of Malfi' well
performed, but Betterton and Ianthe to perfection. (ii, 348)

2 November 1666: ...and so home, I reading all the way to
make end of the 'Bondman' (which, the oftener I read, the
more I like) and begun 'The Duchess of Malfi' which seems
a good play. (vi, 481)

6 November 1666: ...after dinner down alone by water to
Deptford, reading 'Duchess of Malfi' the play, which is
pretty good. (vi, 53)

25 November 1668: ...my wife and I to the Duke of York's
house to see 'The Duchess of Malfi', a sorry play, and sat
with little pleasure for fear of my wife's seeing me look
about, and so I was uneasy all the while, though I desire
and resolve never to give her trouble of that kind more.
(viii, 165)

12 May 1669: ...my wife and I to the Duke of York's playhouse, and there, in the side balcony over against the

music, did hear but not see, a new play, the first day
acted, 'The Roman Virgin' an old play and but ordinary I
thought; but the trouble of my eyes with the light of the
candles did almost kill me. (viii, 322)

10.   LANGBAINE'S WEBSTER

1691

From 'An Account of The English Dramatick Poets. Or,
Some Observations and Remarks on the Lives and Writings
of all those that have Published either Comedies, Tragedies ... in the English Tongue'.
   Gerard Langbaine (1656-92) was a son of the Provost of
Queen's College, Oxford, and spirited amateur of the
drama. In the 'Account', Langbaine recorded titles of
over a thousand plays and short accounts of over two
hundred authors, providing a bedrock upon which later
historians would build. Often happily cavalier in his
approach (Thomas Southerne is 'An Author of whom I can
give no further Account, than that he has two plays in
print'), nevertheless his entry on Webster held good for
over a century, and even F.L. Lucas was able to add only
a few details by 1927.

John Webster

An Author that liv'd in the Reign of King James the
First; and was in those Days accounted an Excellent Poet.
He joyn'd with Decker, Marston, and Rowley, in several
Plays; and was likewise Author of others, which have even
in our Age gain'd Applause: As for Instance, Appius and
Virginia, Dutchess of Malfy, and Vittoria Corrombona; but
I shall speak of these in their Order.
   Appius and Virginia, a Tragedy, printed (according to
my Copy) 4°. Lond. 1659. I suppose there may be an older
Edition than mine; but this is that which was acted at
the Duke's Theatre, and was alter'd (as I have heard by
Mr. Carthwright) by Mr. Betterton: For the Plot, consult
Livy, Florus, &c.
   Devil's Law-case, or When Women go to Law, the Devil
is full of business; a Tragi-comedy, approvedly well acted

by Her Majesty's Servants; printed 4°. London. 1623. and
dedicated to Sir Thomas Finch. An Accident like that of
Romelio's stabbing Contarino out of Malice, which turned
to his preservation, is (if I mistake not) in Skenkius his
Observations: At least I am sure, the like happened to
Phaereus Jason, as you may see in Q. Val. Maximus, lib. 1.
cap. 8. The like Story is related in Goulart's Histoires
Admirables, tome 1. page 178.

Dutchess of Malfy, a Tragedy presented privately at
the Black-fryars, and publickly at the Globe, by the King's
Majesty's Servants; and I have seen it since acted at the
Duke of York's Theatre. 'Twas first printed 4°. Lond.
1623, and dedicated to the Right Honourable George, Lord
Berkeley, and since reprinted 4°. Lond. 1678. For the
Plot, consult Bandello's Novels in French, by Belleforest,
N. 19. Beard's Theatre of God's Judgments, Book 2. Ch. 24.
The like Story is related by Goulart, in his Histoires
admirables de notre temps, p. 226.

White Devil, or the Tragedy of Paulo Giordano Ursini,
Duke of Brachiano; with the Life and Death of Vittoria
Corombona, the Famous Venetian Curtezan: acted by the
Queen's Majesty's Servants, at the Phoenix in Drury-lane;
printed 4°. Lond. 1612. and since acted at the Theatre-
Royal, and reprinted 1665.

Besides these plays, our Author has been assisted by
Mr. Rowley in two Others; which because he had the least
part in their Composition, I place to our Author; viz.

Cure for a Cuckold, a Comedy several times acted with
great applause; printed 4°. Lond. 1661.

Thracian Wonder, a Comical History several times acted
with great applause; printed quarto Lond. 1661.

Mr. Philips has committed a great Mistake, in ascribing
several Plays to our Author, and his Associate Mr. Decker;
One of which belong to another Writer, whose Name is
annexed, and the rest are Anonymous: As for Instance,
The Noble Stranger, was writ by Lewis Sharpe; and The
New Trick to cheat the Devil, Weakest goes to the wall,
and Woman will have her will, to unknown Authors.

11. ON THE FAILURE OF BIRTH CONTROL IN 'THE DUCHESS OF
MALFI' AND 'HENRY VIII'

1698

An anonymous author admits that drama can succeed despite
violation of the unities, but Webster and Shakespeare
wanted art in two of their plays. From 'A Defence of
Dramatick Poetry: Being a Review of Mr. Collier's View,
London 1698'. Mr Collier is, of course, Jeremy Collier,
whose 'Short View of the Immorality and Profaneness of the
English Stage' appeared earlier in the same year. From
'The Shakespearean Allusion Book', ed. John Munro (1932),
pp. 412-13.

'Tis true, I allow thus far, That it ought to be the chief
care of the Poet, to confine himself into as narrow a
Compass as he can, without any particular stint, in the
two First Unities of Time and Place; for which end he
must observe two Things. First upon occasion (suppose in
such a Subject as Mackbeth) he ought to falsifie even
History it self. For the Foundation of that Play in the
Chronicles, was the Action of 25 Years: But in the Play
we may suppose it begun and finish'd in one third of so
many Months. Young Malcom and Donalbain, the Suns of
Duncomb, are but Children at the Murder of their Father,
and such they return with the Forces from England to revenge his Death: whereas in the true Historick Length
they must have set out Children and return'd Men. Secondly,
the length of Time, and distance of Place required in the
Action, ought to be never pointed at, nor hinted in the
play. For example, neither Malcomb nor Donalbain must
tell us, how long they have been in England to raise those
Forces, nor how long those Forces have been Marching into
Scotland; not Mackbeth how far Schone and Dunsinane lay
asunder. By this means the Audience, who come both willing
and prepar'd to be deceiv'd, (populus vult decipi), and
indulge their own Delusion, can pass over a considerable
distance both of Time and Place unheeded and unminded, if
they are not purposely thrown too openly in their way, to
stumble at. Thus Hamlet, Julius Caesar, and those Historick Plays shall pass glibly; when the Audience shall
be almost quite shockt at such a Play as Henry the 8th. or
the Dutchess of Malfey. And why, because here's a Marriage
and the Birth of a Child, possibly in two Acts; which points

so directly to Ten Months length of time, that the Play
has very little Air of Reality, and appears too much unnatural. In this case therefore 'tis the Art of the Poet
to shew all the Peacocks Trains, but as little as possible
of her Foot.

12. NAHUM TATE REWRITES 'THE WHITE DEVIL'

1707

Extracts from Act I, scene i and Act II, scene i of
'Injur'd Love, or, The Cruel Husband' by Nahum Tate (1652-
1715). Tate, appointed poet laureate in 1692 and the successful adapter of 'King Lear' in 1681, in this instance
failed to see his unacknowledged plagiarism rewarded: the
title-page describes 'Injur'd Love' as 'designed to be
acted at the Theatre Royal'; no record exists that it ever
was. Although many scenes follow in Websterian order, yet
often with laundered lines, Tate introduces a major change
for his post-Restoration intended audience: Vittoria,
though high-spirited and attracted to Brachiano, remains
faithful to Camillo and, as seen below, tells Brachiano
not of her 'foolish idle dream' but of Isabella's virtue.
Thus her 'innocence-resembling boldness', as Lamb later
put it, becomes at the trial the boldness indeed of innocence. And at Brachiano's effort to destroy his marriage,
audiences in an age of decorum were to have heard the
earth groan. Among the missing are the scenes of the
dirge and at the house of convertities, a dumb show (Camillo's death), disgressions, asides, and, in all, the
atmosphere of 'The White Devil'.

[From Act I, scene i]

                                        Enter Brachiano

Bra. Believe me I could wish Time would stand still,
      And never end this Interview—
      Let me into your Bosom, dearest Charmer,
      Pour out instead of Eloquence, my Passion?
      Loose me not Madam, for if you forgoe
      Me, I'm lost indeed.

Vitt. Sir in way of Charity I wish you Heart's ease.

Bra. You are a sweet Physician.

Vitt. Sure deadly Cruelties in Ladies,
      Are as to Doctors many Funerals;
      It takes away their Credit.

Bra. Excellent Creature,
      We call the Cruel, Fair; what Name for you,
      That are so Merciful?

Zan. See now they Close.

Fla. I apprehend you;
      When Principals engage, 'tis scandalous
      For Seconds to be Idle.

Vitt. You call'd me your Physician, and I make
      This Visit to prescribe your Grief a Cure;
      A certain speedy Cure.

Bra. That's double Charity.

Vitt. 'Tis Resolutely at once to quench and stifle
      This hopeless Passion.

Bra. That's too rough a Method,
      And suits not with my Constitution.
      These Minutes are too Precious——

Vitt. Sir, I know their Value,
      And shall improve 'em to our mutual Benefit;
      'Twas I that purpos'd in this Interview,
      We now are wander'd to the brink of Ruin,
      And must turn short, or perish.

Bra. Where's the Danger?

Vitt. It was my Lot
      To be high born and bred, and then reduc'd
      To Fortune's Ebb, and (to compleat my Woes)
      Made Hymen's Martyr, Wedded to Aversion;
      Yet still the name of Husband's Venerable;
      My Vow was Sacred, and let Hope forsake me
      When first——

Bra. Hold; 'twas no Match,
      And I pronounce it void; unnatural Contracts
      Dissolve themselves.

                   [Enter Cornelia observing them at a Distance.

Vitt. Yours was at least Religious;
       You have a Princess, Sir, the Pride of Nature,
       And Paradise of Virtues, worth your Prizing
       If Monarch of the World;   and Sir, this Charmer,
       Your Lover, and almost your Worshipper.

Cor.   My fears are fall'n upon me!   Oh my Heart,
       My Son, their Pandar?

Vitt. Beware my Lord! Orphans and Widows cries,
       Defrauded Labour's starving Sighs are loud;
       But none, to draw down Vengeance from Above,
       No! None like the Complaints of injur'd Love.

Bra.   You have both said and answer'd, call'd her Wife
       And mine.

Vitt. So are your Dukedoms, Sir — I own these Beauties
       Mean as my Fortune, yet above the Purchase
       Of Crowns and Scepters; brighter too than they,
       While deck't with Innocence — that Jewel lost
       The Mountain Nymph that dresses at a Fountain
       Her inn'cent Head with Daisies,would outshine me
       Blazing with diamonds. [Cornelia comes near to 'em.

Bra.   Content, and who shall dare to call it a Crime?

Vitt. Were Censure aw'd, what Troops can you Command,
       What Guards to silence the Accuser here/
       The rev'ling gaudy Scene in time will change.
       Furies succeed the flatt'ring Cupid's fled,
       And howling Honor haunt the guilty Bed.

[From Act II, scene i]

Isa.   Had I, who am the Sufferer,
       Been the offender, this submissive Posture
       Might plead a Pardon and prevail——
       Behold, my Lord, upon her humble Knees
       Your injured Wife suing for Reconcilement!
       Return to me, and to your self return;
       Shake off this sullen Cloud and shine again
       The dazzling Wonder of the World; return,
       If not to me, to Fame, Content, and Quiet.

Bra.   Content and Quiet!   'Twas for that I left

My haunted House and see! The Goblin follows me.
I cry ye mercy; you are Flesh and Blood,
Your Business, Assignation with some Gallant,
That must supply our Discontinuance....

Bra. Your hand I'le kiss.
      This is the last Ceremony of my Love,
      Henceforth I'le never Bed with you; be this my Witness,
      This Wedding Ring; I'le ne'er more sleep with you——
      And this Divorce shall be as duly kept,
      As if the Judge had doom'd it; Fare you well,
      Our Sleeps are sever'd.

Isa. Forbid it, the sweet Union
      Of all Things sacred; why the listning Stars
                              [A Noise under Ground.
      Will start at this! The Stars! Earth groan'd
        to hear it.
      Is it firm Ground we tread——
      Or the Convulsion here——
                     [laying her Hand at her Breast.

Bra. Let not thy Love
      Make thee an Unbeliever, this my Vow
      Shall never on my Life be disannul'd
      By Recantation, let thy Brother Rage
      Beyond a Lapland Tempest, a Sea Fight,
      My Vow is fix'd.

Isa. O my Winding Sheet!
      For I shall need thee shortly, dear my Lord,
      Let me hear once more, what I wou'd not hear; never?

Bra. Never.   [Lightning and Thunder.

13. LEWIS THEOBALD REWRITES 'THE DUCHESS OF MALFI'

1733

Extracts from (a) the Preface to 'The Fatal Secret' (London, 1735), by Lewis Theobald (1688-1744), staged at Covent
Garden on 4 and 6 April 1733; and (b) 'The Fatal Secret',

IV, i and V, iv (the torture of the Duchess and the last
scene).
    Theobald, Shakespearean editor, translator, playwright,
and Pope's original King of Dullness, provides us in his
Preface with our one piece of neo-classic criticism of
Webster, and in the play itself with a triumphantly wrong-
headed example of imposing the classic unities and decorous
rhetoric upon a dark play never meant for such illumination.
With the regularization of the plot (no children are born,
among other changes), scenes are lost or rewritten, simplicity replaces complexity, and the Duchess is allowed to
live. Webster's play, in the process, dies.

(a) The Importunity of some Friends whom I could no means
disobey has drawn from me the Publication of the Piece
at a Disadvantage.... Such was its fate ... that, appearing
at a Season when the Weather was warm and the Town in a
political Ferment, it was praised and forsaken; and I had
the choice Comfort left me of hearing everybody wonder that
it was not supported.... Though I called it 'The Fatal
Secret' I had no Intention of disguising from the Public
that (as my friend has confessed for me in the Prologue)
John Webster had preceded me, above a hundred years ago,
in the same story. I have retained the names of the Characters in his 'Duchess of Malfi', adopted as much of his
Tale as I conceived for my Purpose, and as much of his
Writings as I could turn to account without giving into
too obsolete a Diction. If I have borrowed Webster's
Matter freely I have taken it up on fair and open Credit,
and hope I have repaid the Principal with Interest. I
have nowhere spared myself out, of Indolence; but have
often engrafted his Thoughts and Language because I was
conscious I could not so well supply them from my own
Fund. When I first read his scenes I found something
singularly engaging in the Passions, a mixture of the
Masculine and the Tender which induced me to think of
modernizing them. Another Motive was that the distress
of the Tale was not fictitious but founded upon an authentic Record....
    As to our countryman Webster, though I am to confess
Obligations to him I am not obliged to be blind to all his
Faults. He is not without his incidents of Horror, almost
as extravagant as those of the Spaniard [Lope de Vega].
He had a strong and impetuous Genius, but withal a most
wild and undigested one; he sometimes conceived nobly
but did not always express with Clearness; and if he now
and then soars handsomely he as often rises into regions

of bombast; his Conceptions were so eccentric that we
are not to wonder why we cannot trace him. As for Rules,
he either knew them not or thought them too servile a
Restraint. Hence it is he skips over Years and Kingdoms
with an equal Liberty. It must be [admitted] the Unities
were very sparingly observed at the Time in which he wrote;
however, when any Poet travels too fast that the Imagination of his Spectators cannot keep pace with him, Probability is put quite out of Breath. Nor has he been less
licentious in another Respect: He makes mention of
Galileo and Tasso, neither of whom were born till near
half a Century after the Duchess of Malfi was murdered.

Having been so free in characterizing the old Bard, I
may reasonably expect an inquisition into my own Performance. But I am willing to be beforehand with Censurers
and allow all the Faults they shall think fit to impute
to it. What I have done is submitted to Examination and
I'll spare myself the Odium of marking it out. If the
piece has any Praise it is, in my opinion, that it had
Pow'r to draw tears from fair Eyes. The Poet who writes
for the Stage, should principally aim at pleasing his
female Judges; for the best Proof whether he can draw a
distress is how far their Nature and Virtues are touched
with his Portrait.

(b) Ferd. Where are you?

  Dutch. Here, sir.

  Ferd. This Darkness suits, and pictures out your Fortune.
From what a Blaze of Glory, where you sate
Inshrin'd a Wonder, has your hapless Conduct
Sunk you in Shade! It fares with erring Greatness,
As with that Vapour call'd a shooting Star;
Which, bright in Passage, yet, once fall'n, becomes
Unlustrous as the Earth with which it mixes.

  Dutch. Alas! I feel my Fault, and find this Gloom,
Like to the sudden Darkness of a Storm,
Shew me my Danger. — But, my gracious Brother,
Make not my willful Trespass your Discomfort:
But let the Affliction, as the Punishment,
Fall singly on my self.

  Ferd. ——It cannot be:
You were the Sun, the Splendour of our House,
And I, like the foolish Indian, gaz'd
Almost with Adoration of your Brightness,

Am chill'd, and darken'd, by your fading Ray.
My lustre is impaired; my Titles sullied;
And the rude Finger of Contempt shall mark me
As Brother to the wanton, widow'd Malfy,
Who married with her Groom.

    Dutch. Sure, that Reproach
Is of the Bitt'rest.

    Ferd. Come, no more of this,
I mean to seal my Peace: Approach yet nearer:
Where is your Hand?

    Dutch. Here, Sir; but let me Kneel,
And print a Kiss on yours of true Affection.

    Ferd. Hold, you're too lib'ral in these Acts of Fondness.
Know, that your son this Night arrives from Naples;
And, with the Morrow's Dawn, I'm for Calabria.
Here, wear this Ring; and keep it as the Warrant,
To judge how Time, and your repentant Sorrows
May help to work our farther Reconcilement.

    Dutch. Now blessings on your heart!

    Ferd. Lights for the Dutchess——
        [Duke Ferdinand flings away; and enter Urbino and
                            Servants with Lights.

    Dutch. Dear Pledge of Peace! More welcome to me far
Than Pardon to a Wretch condemn'd: — Start, eyes!
Leap from thy Seat at once, unfeeling Sense;
And instant Frenzy take up all my Brain!
What horrid Magick's bound in this dread Circle,
To shake me thus with Fears? — It is the Ring
I gave Antonio, when he parted from me.

    Urb. It is; and he returns it, firm to Promise,
'Tis the last Legacy his falt'ring Tongue
Bequeathed you at his Death.

    Dutch. Distraction! Horror!
Thy words are Keen as Daggers to my Heart;
His Death! — O dear Antonio, art thou dead?
Has all my pious Care then been in vain,
To snatch thee from these fell Barbarians' Fury?
There is not betwixt Heav'n and Earth one
I stay for now. — Say, wilt thou seek these Tygers
And in a Sister's Name implore one Grant,
Which I'll account as Mercy?

Urb. What's your Boon?

Dutch. That they would bind me to his lifeless Trunk,
'Til I'm a Corse like him.

[Ferdinand soliloquizes after the Duchess has been led
offstage to her presumed death.]

Ferd. O sacred Innocence, that sweetly sleeps
On Turtles' Feathers; whilst a guilty Conscience
Makes all our Slumbers worse than fevrish Dreams,
When only monstrous Forms disturb the Brain.
'Tis a black Register, wherein are writ
All our good Deeds and bad: A Perspective,
That shows us Hell more horrid than Divines,
Or Poets, know to paint it. — Hark, what Noise?
The Screams of Women, ever and anon,
Ring thro my Ears; shrill as the Cries they send,
When the stern Murth'er takes 'em unprepar'd. —
A thousand fancied Horrors shake my Soul,
E'er since I dictated this Deed of Slaughter.
There is no written Evidence to proclaim
My Order; and must coward Apprehension
Give it a Tongue? — The Element of Water
Drops from the Clouds, and sinks into the Earth;
But Blood flies upward, and bedews the Heav'ns. —
The Wolf shall find her Grave, and scrape it up,
Not to devour the Corse, but to discover
The horrid Murther. — Shall I let her live?
What says Revenge to that? Or what says Nature?
Resentment whispers Treason still to Virtue,
And, to repent us of a blameful Purpose,
Is manly pious Sorrow. — She shall live.
                    [As the Duke is going out, enter Bosola.
Where is my Sister?

Bos. She's what you would have her.

Ferd. I say, where is she? I would see my Sister.

Bos. Set wide these folding Doors. — There fix your Eye.
      [The scene draws, and discovers the Dutchess in her
      Coffin. The Cord lying upon it.

Ferd. Ha! Thou too fatally obedient Traytor!
Is she then dead? Is Mercy sprung too late?
Cover her Face; my Eyes begin to dazzle.

[In the final scene, at the Royal Monument, Ferdinand and the Cardinal fatally wound one another, and the Cardinal, not Bosola, speaks of dying 'In a mist; I know not how'. Antonio, Bosola, Pescara, Delio, the young Duke of Malfi, and others arrive at the monument-tomb to hear the Cardinal's last words and to learn that the body of the Duchess is not in the tomb. Bosola has 'cheated / Her credulous Brother with a waxen Image: / That beauteous Waxen Image so admir'd / Framed by Vincentio di Laureola / When her Grace married first'. Bosola promises to produce the hidden corpse as an act of clemency and leaves the stage. Then shouts are heard.]

Pesc. What Shouts of Joy are these, that rend the Air?
Again, a nearer sound. — Oh my Liege,
By my best Hopes, my Royal Mistress lives:
Oh, virtuous Bosola!

Ant. —————Amazing transport!

[Enter Bosola, follow'd by the Dutchess, Cariola, and Attendants in Mourning. The Young Duke runs, and embraces her.

Duke. My Mother! O, what Words can speak my Joy?
Let my Tears answer for my Heart's big Pleasure.
What Miracle has giv'n you back to Life?

Dutch. This Man, appointed to my Death, preserv'd me.
[To Bosola, who kneels.

Duke. Oh think, what Honours can requite Thy Virtue.

Dutch. Preserv'd me from a Fate, had giv'n me Peace,
But now I'm doom'd the Slave to lasting Sorrows:
A mourning Widow, past the Help of Comfort,
For poor Antonio's loss.

Bos. Even there I'm pleas'd
To lend a Dawn of Hope. That fatal Ring,
Which you suppos'd sent from your murther'd Lord,
Came from his Hand t'assure you of his Safety.
A Pilgrim brought it; gave it to your Servants;
But, intercepted by your cruel Brother,
'Twas used in Aggravation of your Tortures.

Duke. Be still the Messenger of farther Comfort,
And heighten, if thou canst, thy countless Merit
Ten thousand Ducats crown the virtuous Man,
Who brings Antonio to us.

Ant. O my Princess!
Look up, and once more bless the lost Antonio.
　　[Throws down his Pilgrim's Staff, and opens his frock.

Dutch. 'Tis He! — O Ecstasy, too strong for Sense!
Joy crowds about my Heart in such Excess,
The Torrent quite o'er-bears me.

Ant. Excellent Creature!
Cleave to my heart. O Bosola! My Brother!
Still wear that Title: and divide in all
My Wealth; all Joys, but One, the Sum of All.

Dutch. They now no more shall part us.

Ant. ——Never, never:
Our Foes are past a Fear. — My dearest Prince,
Accept my duteous Knee.

Duke. O rise, Antonio:
My Father and my Friend! — I am too young
To hold the veins of Pow'r: Be thou my Guide;
And teach the State to ven'rate more thy Virtues.
What other Pilgrim's that?

Ant. 'Tis Delio, Sir,
The willing Foll'wer of my wayward Fortunes.

Duke. That Service shall command him to Reward.
Come, Madam, to the Palace, still your own:
Where let the Triumphs of your Nuptials banish
The Mem'ry of all Griefs.

Dutch. Some Tears are due
T'appease th' offended Pow'rs. Had I not breath'd
A guilty Vow, my Brothers had not bled.
Till Penitence shall erase that Debt of Sorrow,
I must not yield to Joy.

Pesc. My gracious Mistress,
Permit your old, your faithful Slave to kneel,
And gratulate your strange and unhop'd Rescue.
That Vow but led, to what the Powr's thought fit,
Where Guilt provok'd, the vengeful Shaft is lit.
Thro' Means, beyond what Reason's Eye foresees,
Wise Providence asserts its own Decrees:
Making its Judgments, and Rewards, declare,
That Virtue still is Heav'n's peculiar Care.

14. CHARLES LAMB: WEBSTER RECLAIMED

1808

Charles Lamb (1775-1834) remains the critic who first
looked closely at Webster, at the plays as literature,
thus removing the dramatist from the possession of the
booksellers and anthologists. His 'Specimens of English
Dramatic Poets who lived about the time of Shakespeare'
(1808) was understandably not a popular success; yet it
had the effect of revitalizing the dramatists through
Lamb's enthusiastic, impressionistic appreciation. We
are taken on a tour of the writers, and are shown 'scenes
of passion, often of deepest quality', and in Webster's
case, this scenic route proved salutary. Critics have
since noted Lamb's debt to the antiquarians and anthologists; T.S. Eliot would later fault Lamb for setting
in motion the fatal idea that to the word-lover, drama
and poetry are two separate things (Four Elizabethan
Dramatists, 'Selected Essays', 1934). Indeed, Swinburne
and Gosse refer to Webster's 'poems'. Nevertheless, we
remain in Lamb's debt: Dyce's edition would follow afterwards, and Lamb's critical observations, often in a single
sentence, would provide arguing points for critics into
the twentieth century.
      Lamb quotes first from 'The Devil's Law Case' (I, i;
II, i; V, iv), and from 'Appius and Virginia' (IV, i).
From 'The Duchess of Malfi' he includes the Duchess—
Antonio wedding scene (I, ii); two fables (the Salmon,
III, v, and Reputation, Love, and Death, III, ii); the
Duchess's 'Fie upon this single life' (III, ii); and the
torture and death scenes of the Duchess (IV, i, ii). He
records, from 'The White Devil', Vittoria's trial scene
(III, i); Marcello's death (V, ii); Cornelia's grief
and dirge (V, ii); and various sententiae, noting on
occasions Webster's debt to Shakespeare. The notes following are on (a) the arraignment of Vittoria, (b) Cornelia's dirge, and (c) the tortures of the Duchess. From
the 'Specimens' in 'The Works of Charles and Mary Lamb',
ed. E.V. Lucas (1904), IV, pp. 190, 179.

(a) This White Devil of Italy sets off a bad cause so
speciously, and pleads with such an innocence-resembling
boldness, that we seem to see that matchless beauty of
her face which inspires such gay confidence into her;   and

are ready to expect, when she has done her pleadings,
that her very judges, her accusers, the grave ambassa-
dors who sit as spectators, and all the court, will rise
and make proffer to defend her in spite of the utmost
conviction of her guilt; as the shepherds in 'Don
Quixote' make proffer to follow the beautiful shepherdess
Marcela 'without reaping any profit out of her manifest
resolution made there in their hearing'.

So sweet and lovely does she make the shame,
Which, like a canker in the fragrant rose,
Does spot the beauty of her budding name!

(b) I never saw anything like this Dirge, except the Ditty
which reminds Ferdinand of his drowned father in 'The
Tempest'. As that is of the water, watery; so this is
of the earth, earthy. Both have that intenseness of feeling, which seems to resolve itself into the elements which
it contemplates.

(c) All the several parts of the dreadful apparatus with
which the Duchess's death is ushered in, are not more remote from the conceptions of ordinary vengeance, than the
strange character of suffering which they seem to bring
upon their victims is beyond the imagination of ordinary
poets. As they are not like inflictions *of this life*, so
her language seems not *of this world*. She has lived among
horrors till she is become 'native and endowed unto that
element'. She speaks the dialect of despair, her tongue
has a snatch of Tartarus and the souls in bale. — What
are 'Luke's iron crown', the brazen bull of Perillus,
Procrustes' bed, to the waxen images which counterfeit
death, to the wild masque of madmen, the tomb-maker, the
bellman, the living person's dirge, the mortification by
degrees! To move a horror skillfully, to touch a soul
to the quick, to lay upon fear as much as it can bear, to
wean and weary a life till it is ready to drop, and then
step in with mortal instruments to take its last forfeit —
this only a Webster can do. Writers of an inferior genius
may 'upon horror's head horrors accumulate', but they cannot do this. They mistake quantity for quality, they
'terrify babes with painted devils', but they know not
how a soul is capable of being moved; their terrors want
dignity, their affrightments are without decorum.

15. REACTIONS TO LAMB

1809

Extracts from (a) the 'Monthly Review', LVIII (1809), p.
356; (b) the 'Annual Review, and History of Literature',
VII (1809), p. 568.
The latter is of ɔɔpecial interest as it may be the
work of Coleridge: Lamb, in a letter to him on 7 June
1809, wrote, 'I am also obliged, I believe, for a review
in the "Annual", am I not?' ('Letters', ed. E.V. Lucas
(1935), III, p. 73). Coleridge, as best we know, is silent
on the matter. Although the review is favourable, ending
with high praise for Lamb and his 'kindred power' with the
Elizabethans, the reviewer anticipates Archer in 1893 as to
Webster's handling of horror.

(a) The notes before us, indeed, have nothing very remarkable, except the style, which is formally abrupt, and
elaborately quaint. Some of the most studied attempts to
display excessive feeling we had noted for animadversion
but the task is unnecessary. We will not even say a word
of comparison made between the *Dirge* in the White Devil,
and the *Ditty* in Shakespeare's Tempest, 'the one of the
earth, earthy, the other of the water, watery: both have
that *intenseness of feeling* which seems *to resolve itself
into the elements* which it contemplates'; —— nor will we
discuss 'the dilaceration of the spirit and the extentera-
tion of the inmost mind' sustained by the light-heeled
Calantha, or the 'dignified terms and *decorous* affrightments' which have *bewilderd* Mr. Lamb into such unqualified
and exaggerated admiration of the Duchess of Malfy. Such
phrases may possibly have been adopted for their resemblance to the theatrical language of those times, and un-
questionably the resemblance exists: — but the language
imitated is that of Pistol and Holofernes, or the mock-
heroics of the play-king in Hamlet....

(b) The Duchess of Malfy is one of those plays which Mr.
Lamb admires most warmly, yet surely it contains nothing
half so fine as the praise he has misbestowed upon it....
There is something as absurd as it is monstrous in what is
thus commended. The brother of the duchess, to punish her
for marrying an inferior, torments her with masks and

mockeries of cruelty, waxen images representing the dead
bodies of her husband and children are exhibited;   madmen
are turned loose to dance before her to mad music;   a coffin, cords, and bell are produced;   the grave-digger comes
in: and lastly she is strangled.   Is this moving a horror
skilfully!   The surgeon may as well be called a great master of the passions, for giving pain when he cuts to the
quick, as a dramatist who can employ such means as these.

16.   NATHAN DRAKE RANKS THE ELIZABETHANS

1817

Nathan Drake (1766-1836), essayist and physician, places
Webster after Ford in 'Shakespeare and His Times', pp.
564-5.   Drake, as others, credits Webster with a Shakespearean reach which exceeded his grasp.

'If there be a class of writers of which, above all
others,' observes Mr. Gilchrist, 'England may be proud,
it is of those, for the stage, coeval with and immediately
succeeding Shakespeare';   an observation which the names
alone of Fletcher and Massinger would sufficiently justify;
but when to these we are enabled to add such fellow artists
as Ford, Webster, Middleton, etc. we are astonished that
even the talents of Shakespeare should, for so long a
period, have eclipsed their fame....
    John Webster, whom we shall place immediately after
Ford, as next, perhaps, in talent, resembled him in a predilection for the terrible and strange, but with a cast of
character still more lawless and impetuous.... The tragedies, especially 'The White Devil,' or 'Vittoria Corombona,' first printed in 1612, and 'The Dutchesse of Malfy,'
in 1623, are very striking, though, in many respects, very
eccentric proofs of dramatic vigour.
    It appears however, from the dedication to 'The White
Devil,' that our author was well acquainted with the laws
of the ancient drama, and that 'willingly, not ignorantly,'
he adopted the Romantic or Shakespearean form.

[Quotes the last paragraph from Webster's dedication to
'The White Devil'.]

The silence which modesty dictated to Webster, ought long ago to have been broken by a declaration, that he was fully entitled to a niche in the same temple of Fame with those whom he has here commemorated. In his pictures of wretchedness and despair, he has introduced touches of expression which curdle the very blood with terror, and make the hair stand erect. Of this, the death of 'The Dutchesse of Malfy', with all its preparatory horrors, is a most distinguishing proof. The fifth act of his 'Vittoria Corombona' shows, also, with what occasional skill he could imbibe the imagination of Shakspeare, particularly where its features seem to breathe a more than earthly wildness. The danger, however, which almost certainly attends such an aspiration after, what may be called inimitable excellence, Webster has not escaped; for where his master moves free and etherial, an interpreter for other worlds, he but too often seems laboriously striving to break from terrestial fetters; and, when liberated, he is, not unfrequently, 'an extravagant and erring spirit.' Yet, with all their faults, his tragedies are, most assuredly, stamped with, and consecrated by, the seal of genius.

17. 'BLACKWOOD'S' REVIEWS WEBSTER

1818

John Wilson (1785-1854), frequent contributor to 'Blackwood's' as 'Christopher North' and Professor of Moral Philosophy at Edinburgh, looks backward in his Webster summation to neo-classic standards and, on the character of Vittoria, ahead to Kingsley's unfortunate strictures. Extracts from Analytical Essays on the Early English Dramatists, 'Blackwood's Edinburgh Magazine', III (March and August 1818), pp. 656-62, 557-62. Wilson writes here as 'H.M.' and is reprinted chiefly for the historical record.

...none of the predecessors of Shakespeare must be thought along with him, when he appears before us like Prometheus moulding the figures of men, and breathing into them the animation, and all the passions of life.

The same may be said of almost all his illustrious contemporaries. Few of them ever have conceived a consistent
character, and given a perfect drawing and coloring of it;
they have rarely indeed inspired us with such belief in
the existence of their personages, as we often feel towards
those of Shakespeare, and which makes us actually unhappy
unless we can fully understand every thing about them, so
like are they to living men. And if we wonder at his
mighty genius, when we compare his best plays with all
that went before him, we shall perhaps wonder still more
when we compare them with the finest works of those whose
genius he himself inspired, and who flourished during the
same splendid era of dramatic poetry.

This will hold time with the works of all the great
dramatists of that time, to which the public mind has of
late years been directed — the Fletchers, the Jonsons,
the Massingers, and the Fords. Still more so, is it the
case with those many other men of power which that age,
fruitful in great souls, produced. The plans of their
dramas are irregular and confused, — Their characters
often wildly distorted, — and an air of imperfection and
incompleteness hangs in general over the whole composition; — so that the attention is wearied out, — the
interest flags, — and we rather hurry on, than are hur-
ried, to the horrors of the final catastrophe.

To none of our early dramatists do these observations
more forcibly apply than to Webster. Some single scenes
are to be found in his works inferior in power of passion
to nothing in the whole range of the drama. He was a man
of a truly original genius, and seems to have felt strong
pleasure in the strange and fantastic horrors that rose
up from the dark abyss of his imagination. The vices and
the crimes which he delights to paint, all partake of an
extragavance which, nevertheless, makes them impressive
and terrible, and in the retribution and the punishment
there is a character of corresponding wildness. But our
sympathies, suddenly awakened, are allowed as suddenly to
subside. There is nothing of what Wordsworth calls 'a
mighty stream of tendency' in the events of his dramas,
nor, in our opinion, is there a single character that
clearly and boldly stands out before us like a picture.
This being the case, we shall lay before our readers
merely an outline of the story of this his best play
(Duchess of Malfy) and a few of its finest passages....

Hitherto the chief merit of the drama has consisted in
the delineation of the mutual affection and attachment of
the Duchess and her husband. We have purposely taken no
notice of much low and worthless matter in the subordinate
conduct of the play. There is something very touching and

true to nature in the warmth, yet purity of feeling, that
characterizes the Duchess; and knowing from the first
that fiendish machinations are directed against her peace,
we all along consider her as an interesting object, upon
whom there is destined to fall some fatal calamity. In
the fourth act the tragedy assumes a very different com-
plexion, and the peculiar genius of Webster bursts forth
into strange, wild, fantastic, and terrible grandeur.
The Duchess is sitting in solitary imprisonment, and by
the command of her savage brother Ferdinand, in utter
darkness....

[Quotes from IV, i and ii.]

The interest of the drama thus expires with the fourth
act. In the fifth, there is some powerful painting of the
distraction of Ferdinand, whom remorse has driven into
madness, — and a murderous confusion of death among the
guilty actors; but the extracts already given are sufficient to enable our readers to estimate the general character of the tragedy, and our limits prevent us from offering
any further criticism.

This play ['The White Devil'] is so disjointed in its action, — the incidents are so capricious and so involved, —
and there is, throughout, such a mixture of the horrible
and the absurd — the comic and the tragic — the pathetic
and the ludicrous, — that we find it impossible, within
our narrow limits, to give any thing like a complete analysis of it. All we shall attempt, therefore, will be to
present our readers with such specimens as may serve to
characterize the peculiar genius of Webster.

[The plot of 'The White Devil' is summarized.]

Brachiano on his death-bed is struck with a raving madness, —
and Lodovico and Gaspero having been admitted to him in the
habit of Capuchins, with crucifix and hallowed candle, throw
off their disguise, and insult his dying agonies with re-
proaches and curses.... The whole of this scene is distinguished by that sort of wild, grotesque, fantastical, and
extravagant horror in which the strength of Webster lies —
and which, in spite of ourselves, strikes us with the same
feelings that are produced in real life by some strange and
unnatural murder.
    Previous to this catastrophe, Flamineo, the wicked son
of Cornelia, had, in a fit of demonaical passion, slain
his brother Marcello. Few scenes in dramatic poetry sur-

pass the following in pathos:

[Quotes at length from V, iv, Cornelia's mad scene]...

There is great power in this drama, and even much fine
poetry, but, on the whole, it shocks rather than agitates,
and the passion is rather painful than tragical.   There
are, in truth, some scenes that altogether revolt and disgust, — and mean, abandoned, and unprincipled characters
occupy too much of our attention throughout the action of
the play.   There is but little imagination breathed over
the passions of the prime agents, who exhibit themselves
in the bare deformity of evil, — and scene follows scene
of shameless profligacy, unredeemed either by great intellectual energy, or occasional burstings of moral sensi-
bilities.   The character of Vittoria Corombona, on which
the chief interest of the drama depends, is sketched with
great spirit and freedom, — but though true enough to
nature, and startling by her beauty and wickedness, we
feel that she is not fit to be the chief personage of tragedy, which ought ever to deal only with great passions,
and with great events.   There is, however, a sort of fascination about this 'White Devil of Venice,' which accom-
panies her to the fatal end of her career, — and something
like admiration towards her is awakened by the dauntless
intrepidity of her death.

I will not in my death shed one base tear,
Or if look pale, for want of blood, not fear.

18.   CAMPBELL REFUTES LAMB

1819

Thomas Campbell (1777-1844), poet, critic, and translator,
had Scott's original encouragement in what became a seven-
volume anthology covering several centuries of English
poets.   Although he borrows from Lamb's Webster selection,
he somewhat satirically finds Lamb's judgment faulty.   So,
of course, is Campbell's accuracy: Webster's 'advertisement' ('To the Reader') belongs to 'The White Devil'.   From
'Specimens of the English Poets', III, pp. 215-33.

Langbaine only informs us of this writer, that he was
clerk of St. Andrew's parish, Holborn, and was esteemed
by his contemporaries. He wrote his two comedies, the
Thracian Wonder, and the Cure for a Cuckold, in conjunction with Rowley, Dekker, and Marston. Few other pieces,
entirely his own, are Vittoria Corombona, the tragedy of
Appius, the Devil's Law Case, and the Duchess of Malfy.
From the advertisement prefixed to his Duchess of Malfy,
the piece seems not to have been successful in the representation. The author says, 'that it wanted that which is
the only grace and setting out of a tragedy, a full and
understanding auditory.' The auditory, it may be sus-
pected, were not quite so much struck with the beauty of
Webster's horrors, as Mr. Lamb seems to have been in writing the notes to his Specimens of our old Dramatic Poetry.
In the same preface Webster deprives himself of the only
apology that could be offered for his absurdities as a
dramatist, by acknowledging that he wrote slowly, a circumstance in which he modestly compares himself to Euripides. In his tragedy of the Duchess of Malfy, the duchess
is married and delivered of several children in the course
of five acts.

[Quotes Vittoria's dream, the murder of the Duchess, and
the echo scene.]

19. HAZLITT ON WEBSTER

1819, 1826

William Hazlitt (1778-1830), critic and essayist, lectured
on the Elizabethan dramatists at the Surrey Institute in
November and December of 1819, after consultation with
Lamb earlier in the year. Prepared at Winterslow Hut in
Wiltshire, the lectures sweep through the dramatists in a
style which, as Hazlitt says, 'flows like a river, and
overspreads its banks'. Of interest is Hazlitt's prefer-
ence for 'The White Devil' rather than 'The Duchess of
Malfi', unlike Lamb, and, indeed, the eighteenth century.
   Extracts from (a) 'Lectures Chiefly on the Dramatic
Literature of the Age of Elizabeth' ('Works of William
Hazlitt', ed. P.P. Howe (1931), VI, pp. 240-6) and (b)
Hazlitt's reactions in 1826 to the efforts of Byron as

dramatist in 'The Plain Speaker', On Reason and Imagina-
tions' ('Works', XII, pp. 53-4).

(a) Webster would, I think, be a greater dramatic genius
than Deckar, if he had the same originality; and perhaps
is so, even without it. His White Devil and Duchess of
Malfy, upon the whole perhaps, come the nearest to Shakespear of any thing we have upon record; the only drawback
to them, the only shade of imputation that can be thrown
upon them, by which they lose some color, is, that they
are too like Shakespear, and often direct imitations of
him, both in general conception and individual expression.
So far, there is nobody else whom it would be either so
difficult or so desirable to imitate; but it would have
been still better, if all his characters had been entirely
his own, had stood out as much from others, resting only
on their own naked merits.... Deckar, has, I think, more
truth of character, more instinctive depth of sentiment,
more of the unconscious simplicity of nature; but he does
not, out of his own stores, clothe his subject with the
same richness of imagination, or the same glowing colors
of language. Deckar excels in giving expression to certain
habitual, deeply-rooted feelings, which remain pretty much
the same in all circumstances, the simple uncompounded elements of nature and passion: — Webster gives more scope
to their various combinations and changeable aspects,
brings them into dramatic play by contrast and comparison, flings them into a state of fusion by a kindled
fancy, makes them describe a wider arc of oscillation
from the impulse of unbridled passion, and carries both
terror and pity to a more painful and sometimes unwarrant-
able excess. Deckar is contented with the historic picture
of suffering; Webster goes on to suggest humble imaginings.
In a word, Deckar is more like Chaucer or Boccaccio; as
Webster's mind appears to have been cast more in the mould
of Shakespear's, as well naturally as from studious emula-
tion. The Bellafront and Vittoria Corombona of these two
excellent writers, shew their different powers and turn of
mind. The one is all softness; the other 'all fire and
air.'... This White Devil (as she is called) is made fair
as the leprosy, dazzling as the lightning. She is dressed
like a bride in her wrongs and her revenge. In the trial-
scene in particular, her sudden indignant answers to the
questions that are asked her, startle the hearers. No
thing can be imagined finer than the whole conduct and
conception of this scene, than her scorn of her accusers
and of herself. The sincerity of her sense of guilt

triumphs over the hypocrisy of their affected and official
contempt for it....
    In the closing scene with her cold blooded assassins,
Lodovico and Gasparo, she speaks daggers, and might almost be supposed to exorcise the murdering field out of
these true devils. Every word probes to the quick. The
whole scene is the sublime of contempt and indifference.

[Quotes V, vi, 188-233.]

    Such are some of the *terrible graces* of the obscure,
forgotten Webster. There are other parts of this play
of a less violent, more subdued, and, if it were possible,
even deeper character; such is the declaration of divorce
pronounced by Brachiano on his wife:

    Your hand I'll kiss:
    This is the latest ceremony of my love;
    I'll never more live with you; &c.

which is in the manner of, and equal to, Deckar's finest
things: — and others, in a quite different style of fanciful poetry and bewildered passion; such as the lamentation
of Cornelia, his mother, for the death of Marcello, and the
parting scene of Brachiano, which would be as fine as Shakespear, if they were not in a great measure borrowed from his
inexhaustible store.

[Quotes further Cornelia's reaction of Marcello's death,
V, ii, 27-69; and Brachiano's awareness of his poisoning
V, iii, 12-41.]

    The Duchess of Malfy is not, in my judgment, quite so
spirited or effectual a performance as the White Devil.
But it is distinguishable by the same kind of beauties,
clad in the same terrors. I do not know but the occasional
strokes of passion are even profounder and more Shakespearian; but the story is more laboured, and the horror is
accumulated to an overpowering and unsupportable height.
However appalling to the imagination and finely done, the
scenes of the madhouse to which the Duchess is condemned
with a view to unsettle her reason, and the interview between her and her brother, where he gives her the supposed
dead hand of her husband, exceed, to my thinking, the just
bounds of poetry and of tragedy. At least, the merit is
of a kind, which, however great, we wish to be rare. A
series of such exhibitions obtruded upon the senses or the
imagination must tend to stupify and harden, rather than
to exalt the fancy or meliorate the heart. I speak this

under correction; but I hope the objection is a venial
common-place. In a different style altogether are the
directions she gives about her children in her last struggles;

> I prythee, look thou giv'st my little boy
> Some syrop for his cold, and let the girl
> Say her pray'rs ere she sleep. Now what
>   death you please——

and her last word, 'Mercy,' which she recovers just
strength enough to pronounce; her proud answer to her
tormentors, who taunt her with her degradation and misery — 'But I am Duchess of Malfy still,' — as if the
heart rose up, like a serpent coiled, to resent the indig-
nities put upon it, and being struck at, struck again; and
the staggering reflection her brother makes on her death,
'Cover her face: my eyes dazzle: she died young!'
Bosola replies:

> I think not so; her infelicity
> Seem'd to have years too many.
>   *Ferdinand*: She and I were twins:
> And should I die this instant, I had liv'd
> Her time to a minute.

This is not the bandying of idle words and rhetorical
common-places, but the writhing and conflict, and the
supreme colloquy of man's nature with itself!

(b) Modern tragedy, in particular, is no longer like a
vessel making the voyage of life, and tossed about by the
winds and waves of passion, but is converted into a handsomely constructed steam-boat, that is moved by the sole
expansive power of words. Lord Byron has launched several
of these ventures lately (if ventures they may be called)
and may continue in the same strain as long as he pleases.
We have not now a number of *dramatis personae* affected by
particular incidents and speaking according to their feelings, or as the occasion suggests, but each mounting the
rostrum, and delivering his opinion on fate, fortune, and
the entire consummation of things. The individual is not
of sufficient importance to occupy his own thoughts or the
thoughts of others. The poet fills his page with *grandes
pensees*. He covers the face of nature with the beauty of
his sentiments and the brilliancy of his paradoxes. We
have the subtleties of the head, instead of the workings
of the heart.... As an instance of the opposite style of

dramatic dialogue, in which the persons speak for themselves
and to one another, I will give, by way of illustration, a
passage from an old tragedy, in which a brother has just
caused his sister to be put to a violent death.

Bosola.	Fix your eye here.
Ferdinand.	Constantly.
Bosola.	Do you not weep?
	Other sins only speak; nurther shrieks out:
	The element of water moistens the earth;
	But blood flies upwards and bedews the heavens.
Ferdinand.	Cover her face: mine eyes dazzle; she died young.
Bosola.	I think not so: her infelicity
	seemed to have years to many.
Ferdinand.	She and I were twins:
	And should I die this instance, I had lived
	Her time to a minute.

'Duchess of Malfy', Act IV, Scene 2.

How fine is the constancy with which he first fixes
his eye on the dead body, with a forced courage, and then,
as his resolution wavers, how natural is his turning his
face away, and the reflection that strikes him on her
youth and beauty and untimely death, and the thought that
they were twins, and his measuring his life by hers up to
the present period, as if all that was to come of it were
nothing! I would fain ask whether there is not in this
contemplation of the interval that separates the beginning
from the end of life, of a life too so varied from good to
ill, and of the pitiable termination of which the person
speaking has been the wilful and guilty cause, enough to
'give the mind pause?' Are not the struggles of the will
with untoward events and the adverse passions of others
as interesting and instructive in the representation as
reflections on the mutability of fortune or inevitableness
of destiny, as the passions of men in general? The tragic
Muse does not merely utter muffled sounds: but we see the
paleness on the cheek, and the life-blood gushing from the
heart! The interest we take in our own lives, in our
successes or disappointments, and the *home* feelings that
arise out of these, when well described, are the clearest
and truest mirror in which we can see the image of human
nature.

20. LORD BYRON RESISTS BUT READS

1820, 1821

'I deny that the English have hitherto had a drama at all,'
wrote Byron to Shelley on 4 April 1821 ('Works of Lord
Byron: Letters and Journals', ed. R.E. Prothero (1898-
1901), V, p. 268). Yet Byron was obviously acquainted
with one of 'those turbid mountebanks'.

Extracts (a) from letters to John Murray on 4 January
1821 and 6 July 1820 ('Letters', V, pp. 217, 47); (b) from
a conversation with Thomas Medwin in 1821 ('Medwin's Conversations with Lord Byron', ed. E.J. Lovell, Jr (1966),
p. 139).

(a) ...do not judge me [his 'Marino Faliero'] by your mad
old dramatists, which is like drinking Usquebaugh and then
proving a fountain: yet after all, I suppose that you do
not mean that spirit is a nobler element than a clear spring
bubbling in the sun; and this I take to be the difference
between the Greeks and those turbid mountebanks — always
excepting B. Jonson, who was a Scholar and a Classic.

...I have been the cause of a great conjugal scrape here
[the Guiccioli affair] which is now before the *Pope* (seriously I assure you) and what the decision of his Sanctity
will be no one can predict. It would be odd that having
left England for one Woman (Vittoria Carambana the 'White
Devil' to wit) I should have to quit Italy for another.

(b) 'I have just been reading Lamb's Specimens,' said
he, 'and am surprised to find in the extracts from the old
dramatists so many ideas that I had thought exclusively my
own. Here is a passage, for instance, from "The Duchess
of Malfy," astonishingly like one in my "Don Juan"....
These Specimens of Lamb's I never saw till today. I am
taxed with being a plagiarist when I am least conscious of
being one; but I am very scrupulous. I own, when I have
a good idea, how I came into possession of it.'

21.   SHELLEY'S TASTES

c. 1820

From 'The Life of Percy Bysshe Shelley' by Thomas Medwin,
ed. H.B. Forman (1913), p. 256. One tends to believe the
gossipy Medwin, in this case. In 'The Cenci', written in
1819, the year of Hazlitt's lectures, Shelley, as does
Webster in 'The White Devil', pictures a guilty woman at
a trial who none the less holds our sympathy through her
courage.

Among English plays he was a great admirer of 'The Duchess
of Malfy', and thought the dungeon scene, where she takes
her executioners for allegorical personages, of Torture
and Murder, or some such grim personifications as equal to
anything in Shakespeare, indeed he was continually reading
the Old Dramatists — Middleton, and Webster, Ford and
Massinger, and Beaumont and Fletcher, were the mines from
which he drew the pure and vigorous style that so highly
distinguished 'The Cenci'.

22.   'BARRY CORNWALL' ON WEBSTER

1823

Bryan Proctor (1787-1874) as 'Barry Cornwall' was a popular minor poet and pseudo-Elizabethan dramatist. His
Gothic Webster appeared in a review of Knowles's 'Vir-
ginius' and Beddoes's 'The Bride's Tragedy' in the 'Edinburgh Review', XXXVII (February 1823), pp. 197-8.

Webster was altogether of a different stamp [from Chapman,
'a grave and solid writer' who 'did not possess much skill
in tragedy']. He was an unequal writer, full of a gloomy
power, but with touches of profound sentiment and the deepest pathos. His imagination rioted upon the grave, and
frenzy and murder and 'tortured melancholy' were in his
dreams. A common calamity was beneath him, and ordinary
vengeance was too trivial for his muse. His pen distilled

house, and picked his brain to outvie the horrors of both.
His visions were not of Heaven, nor of the air; but they
came, dusky and earthy, from the tomb, and the madhouse
emptied its cells to do justice to the closing of his
fearful stories. There are few passages, except in Shakespeare, which have so deep a sentiment as the following.
Ferdinand, Duke of Calabria, has caused his sister (the
Duchess of Malfy) to be murdered by Bosola, his creature.
They are standing by the dead body.

[Quotes IV, 'Fix your eye here' to 'I had lived her time
to a minute.']

    We would not be supposed to assert that the writer was
without his faults. On the contrary, he had several: he
had too gloomy a brain, a distempered taste; he was sometimes harsh, and sometimes dull; but he had great sentiment and, not unfrequently, great vigor of expression. He
was like Marlowe with this difference — that as Marlowe's
imagination was soaring, so, on the other hand, was his
penetrating and profound. The one rose to the stars, the
other plunged to the centre; equally distant from the
bare commonplaces of the earth, they sought for thoughts
and images in clouds and depths, and arrived, by different
means, to the same great end.

23. DYCE'S INTRODUCTION TO WEBSTER

1830

_____

Alexander Dyce (1798-1869), the first editor of John Webster, served briefly as a curate in Cornwall and Suffolk,
having entered the church to avoid the East India Company
career planned for him by his father. However, he abandoned the profession in 1825, settling in London to devote
himself to literature. The best of the early Victorian
editors of the Elizabethan dramatists, Dyce culminated his
scrupulous work with his edition of Shakespeare in 1857,
although it is his James Shirley edition of 1833 which remains of major importance. His Webster served as the
standard text for almost a century. Excerpts from Dyce's
introduction to 'The Works of John Webster, Now First
Collected with Some Account of the Author', London (1830),
pp. v-xlll.

_____

Seldom has the biographer greater cause to lament the
deficiency of materials for his task than where engaged
on the life of any of our early dramatists. Among that
illustrious band John Webster occupies a distinguished
place; and yet so little do we know concerning him, that
the present essay must consist almost entirely of an account of his different productions, and of an attempt to
show that he was not the author of certain prose pieces
which have been attributed to his pen....
    In 1607 were given to the press 'The History of Sir
Thomas Wyatt', 'Westward Ho', and 'Northward Ho', — all
which were composed by Webster, in alliance with Dekker.
    That the authors did not superintend the printing of
'Sir Thomas Wyatt' there can be no doubt, as the text is
miserably corrupt; and I am inclined to believe that it
is merely made up from fragments of the drama called 'Lady
Jane', already mentioned in the quotation from Henslowe's
papers.
    'Westward Ho' and 'Northward Ho' (the former of which
was on the stage in 1605, see vol iii, p. 3) are full
of life and bristle, and exhibit as curious a picture of
the manners and customs of the time as we shall anywhere
find. Though by no means pure, they are comparatively
little stained by that grossness from which none of our
old comedies are entirely free. In them the worst things
are always called by the worst names: the licentious and
the debauched always speak most strictly in character;
and the rake, the bawd, and the courtezan are as odious
in representation as they would be if actually present.
But the public taste has now reached the pitch of refinement, and such coarseness is tolerated in our theatres no
more. Perhaps, however, the language of the stage is puri-
fied in proportion as our morals have deteriorated, and we
dread the mention of the vices which we are not ashamed
to practise; which our forefathers, under the sway of a
less fastidious but a more energetic principle of virtue,
were careless of words and only considerate of actions.
    In 1612, the 'White Devil' was printed, a play of extra-
ordinary power. The plot, though somewhat confused, is
eminently interesting, and the action though abounding,
perhaps a little overcharged, with fearful circumstances,
is such as the imagination willingly receives as credible.
What genius was required to conceive, what skill to embody,
so forcible, so various, and so consistent a character as
Vittoria! We shall not easily find, in the whole range
of our ancient drama, a more effective scene than in that
in which she is arraigned for the murder of her husband.
It is truth itself. Brachiano's throwing down his seat,
and then, with impatient ostentation, leaving it behind

him on his departure; the pleader's Latin exordium; the
jesting interruption of the culprit; the overbearing in-
temperance of the Cardinal; the prompt and unconquerable
spirit of Vittoria — altogether unite in impressing the
mind with a picture as strong and diversified as any which
could be received from an actual transaction of real life.
Mr. Lamb, in his 'Specimens of English Dramatic Poets' (the
most tasteful selection ever made from any set of writers),
p. 229, speaks of the 'innocence-resembling boldness of
Vittoria.' For my own part, I admire the dexterity with
which Webster has discriminated between that simple confidence in their own integrity which characterises the
innocent under the imputation of any great offence, and
the forced and practised presence of mind which the hardened criminal may bring to the place of accusation. Vittoria stands before her judges, alive to all the terrors
of her situation, relying on the quickness of her wit,
conscious of the influence of her beauty, and not without
a certain sense of protection, in case of extreme need,
from the interposition of Brachiano. She surprises by
the readiness of her replies, but never, in a single instance, has the author ascribed to her one word which was
likely to have fallen from an innocent person under similar circumstances. Vittoria is undaunted, but it is by
effort. Her intrepidity has none of the calmness which
naturally attends the person who knows that his own plain
tale can set down his adversary; but it is the high-
wrought and exaggerated boldness of a resolute spirit, —
a determination to outface facts, to brave the evidence
she cannot refute, and to act the martyr though convicted
as a culprit. Scattered throughout the play are passages
of exquisite poetic beauty, which, once read by any person
of taste and feeling, can never be forgotten.
    ...In 1623 were published 'The Dutchess of Malfi' (which
must have been acted as early as 1619, see vol. i p. 170)
and 'The Devil's Law-case'. Of the latter of these plays
the plot is disagreeable, and not a little improbable, but
portions of the serious scenes are not unworthy of Webster.
Few dramas possess a deeper interest in their progress,
and are more affecting in their conclusion, than in 'The
Dutchess of Malfi'. The passion of the Dutchess for
Antonio, a subject most difficult to treat, is managed
with intimate delicacy; and, in a situation at great peril
for the author, she condescends without being degraded, and
declares the affection with which her dependant had inspired
her without losing anything of dignity and respect. Her
attachment is justified by the excellence of its object;
and she seems only to exercise the privilege of exalted
rank in raising merit from obscurity. We sympathise from

the first moment in the loves of the Dutchess and Antonio,
as we would in a long standing domestic affection, and we
mourn the more over the misery that attends them because
we feel that happiness was the natural and legitimate
fruit of so pure and rational attachment. It is the wedded
friendship of middle life transplanted to cheer the cold
and glittering solitude of a court: it flourishes but for
a short space in that unaccustomed sphere, and then is
violently rooted out. How pathetic is the scene where
they part never to meet again! And how beautiful and
touching is her exclamation!

> the birds that live i' th' field,
> On the wild benefit of nature, live
> Happier than we, for they may choose their mates,
> And carol their sweet pleasure to the spring!

The sufferings and death of the imprisoned Dutchess haunt
the mind like painful realities; but it is the less necessary to dwell on them here, as no part of our author's
writings is so well known to the generality of readers
as the extraordinary scenes wherein they are depicted.
In such scenes, Webster was on his own ground. His imagination had a fond familiarity with objects of awe and
fear. The silence of the sepulchre, the sculptures of
marble monuments, the knolling of church bells, the cere-
menets of the corpse, and yew that roots itself in dead
men's graves, are the illustrations that most readily present themselves to his imagination. If he speaks of love,
and of the force of human passion, his language is, -

> This is flesh and blood, sir;
> 'Tis not the figure cut in alabaster,
> Kneels at my husband's tomb —

and when we are told that

> Glories, like glow-worms, afar off shine bright
> But look'd to near, have neither heat nor light,

we almost feel satisfied that the glow-worm which Webster
saw, and which suggested the reflection, was sparkling
on the green sod of some lowly grave....
'Appius and Virginia' was printed in 1654. When I consider its simplicity, its deep pathos, its unobtrusive
beauties, its singleness of plot, and the easy unimpeded
march of its story, I cannot but suspect that there are
readers who will prefer this drama to any other of our
author's production.

24. GEORGE DARLEY WRITES OF WEBSTER

1831

From a letter to Allan Cunningham from George Darley
(1795-1846), poet, mathematician, and editor of Beaumont
and Fletcher. Darley was an often caustic critic of the
dramatists of his day.
From 'The Life and Letters of George Darley', ed.
C.C. Abbott (1928, repr. 1967), pp. 97-8.

Indeed, I often say what a superfluous set of people we
are ... to write poetry when there is so much of it in
print unread. Ay, and of better than the pick of us could
execute, if our brains were beaten together. Have you
ever read Webster? Why, my good sir! there are passages
in 'Vittoria Corombona' almost worthy of the Angel Gabriel.
Don't mind what Campbell says - his criticism upon this
author is nearly as strong evidence against his own poetical genius as the 'Pleasures of Hope' is in favour of it.
There are passages in that play every whit as good as - No!
deuce take it, that would be too bad! - Well, Shakespeare
and Milton excepted, there is poetry in Webster superior
to that of any other English author. If you have not 'The
White Devil' by heart, get it.

25. THE 'GENTLEMAN'S MAGAZINE' CONSIDERS WEBSTER

1833

An anonymous critic reacted to Shakespeare and his contemporaries in a series in the 'Gentleman's Magazine'.
The writer emphasizes the terrors of Webster, as did many
in the earlier nineteenth century, but manages a mid-
Victorian attitude in 1833. From The Early English Drama,
No. III, (a) May 1833, pp. 414-17; and (b) June 1833,
pp. 489-92.

(a) What has been observed of our greatest dramatic poet,
holds true no less of many of his rivals or followers.
We may sometimes lament the imperfection of their judgement, and we may wonder at the capriciousness or perverse-
ness of their taste; but their learning was equal to their
purpose. Their object was to produce a strong and effective emotion on minds not very sensitive or highly culti-
vated. They did not want the fine evolutions, and the
skilful and learned movements of the fencer, but the strong
cuts and thrusts of the swordsman....

The Author [Webster], whose works we now possess for
the first time collected, and beautifully and accurately
edited, although his name is not in honour with general
readers, must rank very high among his brethren of the
sock and buskin in the comparative scale of merit. Inferior to Jonson in richness of comic humour, to Fletcher in
gracefulness of fancy and delicacy of sentiment; and far
below Massinger in the conduct of his plot and the consistency of his characters; he far, very far, surpasses
them all in the depth of his pathos, his tragic power,
and his command over the sublime, the terrible and the
affecting. His fancy seems to indulge itself in forming
every fantastic variety of sorrow, and of following up the
miseries of the broken heart even beyond the sanctuary
of the grave. He loves to dwell (old Burton perhaps would
have said, had he drawn Webster's characters) among
scutcheons, and hour-glasses, and coffins, and all the
painful emblems of mortality; an epitaph to him is a joke,
and a sexton is his bedfellow and friend. He has a dagger
more often in his hand than a knife, and he carries a phial
of poison in his pocket.... His genius, like the yew-tree
which he describes, flourishes best where its roots are in
the tomb; but he possesses considerable variety of reflection, and the elegance of imagery. His verse is often harmonious, and his language elevated and select. Of his
comic power we do not think very highly; and the judicious
formation of his plots and arrangement of incidents do not
seem to have been much studied by him. To enable him to
produce a great effect, all lesser advantages give way;
and, like Rembrandt, he throws every thing else into shadow, to bring out his principal incident with greater force
and luster.

The first play we meet with is 'The White Devil, or
Vittoria Corombona,' a drama exhibiting very unusual trains
of thought, deep reflections, and poetical illustrations,
but with a plot disjointed and not well conceived, and with
characters rather seen in parts and fragments, than consis-
tently and clearly developed. The story does not move by
any series of well-directed incidents to its conclusion;

to which must be added the disgusting representation of a
brother being a pander to his sister's dishonour, as in
the person of Flamineo, although we are not unaware how
much this terrific instance of the most utter depravation
is in keeping with the exhibition of the other ungoverned
and tempestuous passions that sweep over the scenes of
this dark and bloodstained tragedy. His absurd quarrel
with his sister, and the murder of Bracciano by throwing
poison in his hat, must be considered blemishes in the
general merit of the play. There is no doubt of the great
tragic power which Webster possessed; but he has much
abused the fertility of his genius. Terror is too strongly
exerted; there is a strange unnatural mixture of levity
and wretchedness, scorn and sorrow, fiendish laughter,
that seems to feed upon the despair and hopelessness of
the defenceless and desolate heart. The defence of Victoria [sic] at her trial has been highly praised. The
present Editor says — 'that in the whole range of our
ancient drama, we shall not find a more effective scene.'
To this opinion we cannot agree. We consider (to take
the first example that strikes us) the defence of Othello
before the Senate far more true to nature, more effective,
and more masterly in its delineations and design. Too
much of time and words, in Victoria's arraignment, is lost
per accidenta. The trial is too long coming to the point.
Matters irrelevant and useless are introduced; the unity
of our interest is disturbed; nor can we agree in the
Editor's ideas of the fine consistency of Victoria's beha-
viour. When she is commended for her 'innocence-resembling
boldness,' we cannot but recollect her parting imprecation:

> 'Die with those pills in your most cursed maw
> should bring you health! a while you sit o' the bench
> Let your own spittle choke you.'

To our mind the most powerful and the most pathetic
scene, is the interview between the guilty and hardened
husband Bracciano and his injured and most gentle Isabella.
We confess, as we read, the pages were wet with our tears....

[The writer quotes briefly from the passage, and reprints
Cornelia's dirge, which has 'all the hopeless distress,
the vague, bewildered terrified sorrow of Ophelia.']

(b) 'The Duchess of Malfi' is the play in which Webster's
tragic powers expand to their full height. To produce the
effect which he desired, the most violent contrasts are
called out, and the most thrilling emotions excited. The

mind is held in fearful suspense; and many varying passions and hopes and fears, are pouring into it from every
quarter. Yet we must not suppose that mere tragic incident
was called in to harass or agonize the mind, unsupported
by other essential constituents of poetry. Webster has
been called, how justly we know not, the Spagnolet of
poetry. Of Spagnolet's painting we have seen not much;
but we should conceive that he did not possess that just
and natural feeling, which led Webster to soften the savage
grandeur of his terrific scenes, and wring the mind, when
overcharged, away from their deep impressions, to less affecting subjects, and give it an interval to recruit its
exhausted powers. Spagnolet brought to his spectors of
death, and his forms of pain, and his instruments of torture, in all their single and terrible nakedness, before
us: but Webster has great resources behind, when terror
has exhausted his magazines of wrath, and emptied his vials
of affliction. There are in this play reflections of the
robust colours, beautiful and varied imagery, thoughts of
fine selection, sweet touching pathos, elegant and playful
sports of the imagination, and poetical images of high refinement. All the scenes, the opening one especially between the Duchess and Antonio, are charming in taste and
feeling. How delicate and womanly is the Duchess' dis-
closure of her love!

        I thank you, gentle love;
    And 'cause you shall not come to me in debt,
    Bring now my steward, here upon your lips
    I sign your Quietus est. This you should have begged.

    Oh! let me shroud my blushes in your bosom,
    Since 'tis the treasury of all my secrets!

How sweetly expressed is her complaint, where in the
commencement of her distress she says,

    The birds that live i' the field
    On the wild benefit of nature, live
    Happier than we; for they may chose their mates,
    And carol their sweet pleasure to the spring.

This is the very spirit of Fletcher. The main defects
in the tragedy, are the want of a properly progressive
interest, arising from a succession of well-arranged
events; the artifice of imposing on the Duchess by figures of her husband and her children (as if dead) is
childish and disgusting; and the outrageous and fiendish
fury of her brothers all through the play is revolting to

our conceptions of justice and natural propriety. But
the head and front of the offending is in the fourth act.
Who but Webster would have thought of opening to us the
interior of Bedlam; and letting loose his lunatics on the
stage? Was there ever such a stage direction as the following — 'Here the dance, consisting of eight madmen,
with *music anserable* there unto.' Then follows the murder
of the Duchess on the stage, the nurse, and all the children, till we sup full of horrors; but the real interest
of the play has ended in the 4th act. All after is but
coarse and common butchery; — and poetical justice is
secured only by means violent and improbable.

'Devil's Law Case' - This play has little in it agree-
able to the fancy, or moving to the passions. It abounds
with wicked devices, great crimes, and worse confessions.
The duel scene between Contarino and Ercole, Mr. Lamb
calls 'the model of a well-managed and gentlemanlike difference.' Which is true, except that it is somewhat too
romantic. The character of Romelio is one of that fiendish
and desperate wickedness, as only can excite horror: a
description of character peculiar to some few writers of
the early stage; and passing far beyond the sober and
legitimate purposes of tragic imitation. In the noble
reflections of human feeling and character in Shakespeare,
cruelty is softened, if not disguised, by its union with
the greater and more elevated passions; it is the tool
which ambition and pride use to attain their ends if
necessary. Macbeth is cruel, as he is ambitious, but in
the plays of Webster and others, cruelty forms the very
staple of the degraded and loathsome beings in whom it
harbors; it is the base ferocity of the assassin, the
minister of hate and avarice and selfishness, without com-
punction, without shame, without remorse, without dignity....

26. A HISTORIAN'S WEBSTER

1839

Extract from 'Introduction to the Literature of Europe in
the Fifteenth, Sixteenth, and Seventeenth Centuries' by
Henry Hallam (1777-1859), English historian and author of
'The Constitutional History of England' (1827). Webster

receives a brief separate treatment in Hallam's chief
effort as literary critic. From the 1873 edition, pp.
122-4.

Webster belongs to the first part of the reign of James.
He possessed very considerable powers and ought to be
ranked, I think, the next below Ford. With less of poetic
grace than Shirley, he had incomparably more vigour, with
less of nature and simplicity than Heywood, he had a more
elevated genius, and a bolder pencil. But the deep sorrows and terrors of tragedy were peculiarly his province.
'His imagination,' says his last editor, 'had a fond familiarity with objects of awe and fear. The silence of the
sepulchre, the sculptures of marble monuments, the knolling of church bells, the cerements of the corpse, the yew
that roots itself in dead men's graves are the illustrations that most readily present themselves to his imagination.' I think this well written sentence a little one
sided, and hardly doing justice to the variety of Webster's
power; but in fact he was as deeply tainted as any of his
contemporaries with the savage taste of the Italian school,
and in the 'Duchess of Malfy' scarcely leaves enough on
the stage to bury the dead.
    This is the most celebrated of Webster's dramas. The
story is taken from Bandello, and has all that accumulation of wickedness and horror which the Italian novelists
perversely described, and our tragedians as perversely
imitated. But the scenes are wrought up with skill, and
produce a strong impression. Webster has a superiority
in delineating character above many of the old dramatists;
he is seldom extravagant beyond the limits of conceivable
nature, we find the guilt, or even the atrocity, of human
passions, but not that incarnation of evil spirits which
some more ordinary dramatists loved to exhibit. In the
character of the Duchess of Malfy herself there wants
neither originality or skill of management, and I do not
know that any dramatist after Shakespeare would have succeeded better in the difficult scene where she discloses
her love to an inferior. There is perhaps a little failure in dignity and delicacy, especially towards the close;
but the Duchess of Malfy is not drawn as an Isabella or
a Portia; she is a love-sick widow, virtuous and true-
hearted, but more intended for our sympathy than our
reverence.
    'The White Devil' or 'Vittoria Corombona', is not much
inferior in language and spirit to the 'Duchess of Malfy';
but the plot is more confused, less interesting, and worse

conducted. Mr. Dyce, the late editor of Webster, praises
the dramatic vigour of the part of Vittoria, but justly
differs from Lamb, who speaks of 'the innocence resembling
boldness' she displays in the trial scene. It is rather
a delineation of desperate guilt, losing in a counterfeited
audacity all that could seduce or conciliate the tribunal.
Webster's other plays are less striking; in 'Appius and
Virginia' he has done perhaps better than any one who has
attempted a subject not on the whole very promising for
tragedy; several of the scenes are dramatic and effective;
the language, as is usually the case with Webster, is written so as to display an actor's talents, and he has followed the received history sufficiently to abstain from any
excess of slaughter at the close. Webster is not without
comic wit, as well as a power of imagination; his plays
have lately met with an editor of taste enough to admire
his beauties, and not very over-partial in estimating them.

27.   THE STUDENTS' WEBSTER

1848

Extract from 'A Complete Manual of English Literature' by
Thomas B. Shaw (1813-62), a Cambridge graduate who became
Lector of English at the University of St Petersburg.
His 'student manuals' were popular and went through several
editions in spite of occasional errors, such as the avail-
ability of 'The Guise'. From the New York 1870 edition,
pp. 163-4.

But perhaps the most powerful and original genius among
the Shakesperian dramatists of the second order is John
Webster. His terrible and funereal muse was Death; his
wild imagination revelled in images and sentiments which
breathe, as it were, the odor of the charnel: his plays
are full of pictures recalling with fantastic variety all
associations of the weakness and futility of human hope
and interest, and dark questionings of our future desti-
nies. His literary physiognomy has something of that dark,
bitter, and woeful expression which makes us thrill in the
portraits of Dante. The number of his known works is very
small: the most celebrated among them is the tragedy of

the 'Duchess of Malfy' (1623); but others are not inferior to that strange piece in intensity of feeling and
savage grimness of plot and treatment. Besides the above
we possess 'Guise or the Massacre of Trana', in which the
St Barthelemy is, of course the main action, the 'Devil's
Law Case', the 'White Devil', founded on the crimes and
sufferings of 'Vittoria Corombona', 'Appius and Virginia';
and thus we see that in the majority of his subjects he
worked by preference in themes which offered a congenial
field for his portraiture of the darker passions and of the
moral torture of their victims. In selecting such revolting themes as abounded in the black annals of medieval
Italy, Webster followed the peculiar bent of his great
and morbid genius; in the treatment of these subjects we
found a strange mixture of the horrible with the pathetic.
In his language there is an extraordinary union of complexity and simplicity: he loves to draw his illustrations
not only from 'skulls, graves, and epitaphs,' but also from
the most attractive and picturesque objects in nature, and
his occasional intermingling of the deepest and most innocent emotion and of the most exquisite touches of natural
beauty produces the effect of the daisy springing up amid
the festering mould of a graveyard. Like many of his contemporaries, he knew the secret of expressing the highest
passion through the most familiar images; and the dirges
and funeral songs which he has frequently introduced into
his pieces possess, as Charles Lamb eloquently expresses
it that intensity of feeling which seems to resolve itself
into the very elements they contemplate. His dramas are
generally composed in mingled prose and verse; and it is
possible that he may have had a share in the production of
many other pieces besides those I have enumerated above.

28. 'THE DUCHESS OF MALFI' ON STAGE

1850

On 20 November 1850, Samuel Phelps (1804-78), producer-
director at the Sadler's Wells Theatre, presented 'The
Duchess of Malfi' as adapted by Richard Hengist (Henry)
Horne (1803-84), poet and dramatist, marking the first
stage performance of 'The Duchess' in over a century.
Although the production received several favourable reviews, we may also note the first appearance of condemna-

tory comment from dramatic critics, marking a divided
response that has accompanied Webster productions well
into the later twentieth century. Nevertheless, the 1850
revival provided the actress Isabella Glyn (1823-89)
with one of her most famous roles and inspired subsequent
productions for several years to come. Glyn herself portrayed the Duchess for eighteen years; both Alice Marriot
and, in America, Emma Waller also had success in the role.
Yet from the mid-nineteenth century, Webster on the stage
has often created more difficulty than Webster in the
study.

Horne's adaptation is considered in the Introduction
to this volume. Excerpts from (a) Horne's Preface, Prologue, and Ferdinand's last moments from the published
version of his play, 1850; (b) 'The Times', London, 21
November 1850, p. 8; (c) the 'Athenaeum', 23 November
1850, pp. 1225-6; (d) the 'Spectator', 23 November 1850,
p. 1113; (e) George Henry Lewes's review in the 'Leader',
30 November 1850, reprinted in his 'Dramatic Essays', ed.
William Archer and Robert Lowe (1896), pp. 118-22. Lewes
(1817-78), journalist, philosophical essayist, and dramatic
critic, antedates the approach of his own later editor,
William Archer.

(a) When I first conceived the idea of bringing 'The
Duchess of Malfi' upon the modern stage, I thought that
a considerable reduction of its length, by the erasure
of a number of unnecessary scenes, and a little revision
of certain objectionable passages, would be nearly sufficient. But, before I had got half through the first act,
the futility of such a course became sufficiently apparent.
Still I hope to accomplish the task, with due reverence to
a work which I considered the most powerful of any tragedy
not in Shakespeare, and equal in that quality even to him.
For, if the two chief elements of tragic power be terror
and pity, assuredly both of these are carried to the highest degree in 'The Duchess of Malfi'.

The more, however, I examined the structure of the
tragedy the more manifest did it become, that the only way
to render it available to the stage must be that of re-
constructing the whole, cutting away all that could not
be used, and filling up the gaps and chasms.

Nor was this all that it required. The contradictions,
incongruities, and oversights were of a kind that exceeded
anything I had previously conjectured. In truth, until I
came to scrutinize the scenes thus closely, I had overlooked these discrepancies as well as the author, and

others have done. Let me give an instance. Antonio sends
off his friend Delio, post-haste to Rome on a service of
most vital importance; and the next time they meet on
Delio's return, Antonio has forgotten all about it. Again:
after the Duchess (in Act IV, Scene i, of the original)
has seen, as she believes, her children lying dead in
their shrouds - she, in the very next scene, has entirely
forgotten this, and gives precise and affecting maternal
directions concerning them both, as if they were alive.
Several other extraordinary instances might be mentioned,
but it would only confuse the mind between the two versions, to specify them and answer no good purpose.
     It hence became apparent that if this great tragedy
was to be exhumed from its comparative obscurity, by representation on the stage, all the characters must be made
consistent with themselves, and all the events proper to
them - all the parts must be made coherent - and all this
be built with direct relationship to the whole, and direct
tendency to the final results. Yet, amidst all this the
great scenes must be religiously preserved, or I should
do worse than nothing, and produce a weak and sacrilegious
deformity. What I have, therefore, sought to do, is as
though a grand old abbey - haunted, and falling into
decay - stood before me, and I had undertaken to re-
construct it anew with as much of its own materials as
I could use - asking pardon for the rest - but preserving
almost entire its majestic halls and archways, its loftiest turrets, its most secret and solemn chamber, where the
soul, in its hours of agony, uplifted its voice to God.
     Writing this Preface the night before performance, when
no one can have certain knowledge of the effect of tragic
scenes so awful, and others so new to the stage, I am
anxious to record that I do not doubt but this tragedy of
Webster's will be worthily acted at Sadler's Wells, not
only by Mr. Phelps, Miss Glyn, and Mr. Bennett, but by
all principals and seconds in the performance. Be the result what it may, my cordial acknowledgments are due to the
careful assiduity, the unwearied energy, and watchfulness
with which a tragedy, so long highly honoured in dramatic
literature, has been placed by Mr. Phelps upon the stage -
to the pains taken by each performer in the rehearsals -
and though I name Mr. T.L. Greenwood last, he stands foremost in his appreciation of the present version of 'The
Duchess of Malfi'.
     In this edition, printed from the prompter's copy, most
of the acting directions are allowed to remain, with a
view to render the numerous stage difficulties less oner-
ous to future managers.

The sun himself, his planets and his peers,
Circling some vaster centre of all spheres:
All *these* again in harmony combine—
Moving for ever, somewhere — by design!

The tree that hath no hope can bear no fruit:
Must stars come down to teach the oak its root?
Show how eternal nature in the earth
From light and air claims a perennial birth;
That while the heart of man remains the same,
The Drama bears within a constant flame,
Ready to light our progress, onward ever,
When *truth* and *power* combine in that endeavour;
Ready to re-illume its ancient stories,
And weave its brow with *new* and lasting glories!

In our fresh period vigourous life requires
More solid food for its exalting fires;
Great passions — doings — sufferings, great hopes still,
To urge us up the steep and thorny hill,
Where genius, science, liberty, combined,
Give lasting empire to the advancing mind.
Wherefore, tonight, we bring the inspiring themes
Of great, old Webster, — clad in whose strong beams
We venture forth on the uplifted sea
Of his invention's high-wrought poesy,
Steering to reach the storm-rent beacon tower,
Trusting his hand — and with full faith in power.

[*The body of* Antonio *is carried in*]
Ferdinand [*bending forward*]: I must look closer at that
    sleeping man.   [*They assist him forward*]
His face is paler than the waxen mould
My sister once did stare at through her tears;
And I do seem to breed strange memories
Of passion and of sorrow in my brain,
Where thunder lately echoed.   [*He kneels beside the body*]
                    Shifting mists
Thicken between us. Poor Antonio—
A damp and heavy earth lies on our hearts—
The frost doth take our knees, so that I pray,
                    [*Taking* Antonio's *hand*]
But cannot rise — my thoughts lose government
And have no meaning — but stray all forlorn,
Seeking forgiveness — till some weeping ghost
Melt us into itself. Marina calls!   [*He dies*]

(b) It has ever been the delight of the present managers
of Sadler's Wells to seek after dramatic curiosities.
Here the less familiar of Shakespeare's plays have been
revived; forgotten works of Beaumont and Fletcher have
been taken from the shelf; and last night a still bolder
attempt was made by the production of the 'Duchess of
Malfi', one of the most celebrated plays of old, strong,
and — we must add — barbarous John Webster....
    Those of our literary critics who have been fascinated
by the vigour of Webster's writing, and his peculiar mastery in awakening sensations of terror, regard the 'Duchess
of Malfi' as his greatest creation. The plot of his work
is simple to the last degree, but the author has filled it
with horror, mental and physical, to its extreme complement.

[The writer recounts the plot and quotes Lamb on the
Duchess's tortures.]

    There is certainly a grandeur about Webster; lines
might be taken from this piece of surpassing strength,
and now and then the depths of human nature are sounded
with a strange sort of instinct. The distich which points
the moral of the whole tale —

    Whether we fall by ambition, blood, or lust,
    Like diamonds we are cut by our own dust,

is of itself a brilliant scintillation of a kind of ghastly
wit. But still we would warn enthusiasts against regarding such a work as the 'Duchess of Malfi' as anything beyond a curiosity. It is, we are ready to admit, a fine spe-
cimen of pristine strength, but let us not be too ready to
take a monument for a model.
    Mr. Horne, a gentleman of high poetical feeling, and
endowed with a peculiar elegance of mind, has accomplished
very skillfully the task of rendering the sanguinary work
of John Webster tolerable on a modern stage, cutting away,
by the by, some of the very horrors which excited Lamb's
admiration. Those who are familiar with the original, and
are acquainted with the rude coarseness of the dialogue
and the atrocities ordered by the stage directions, will
see that he has had no easy problem to solve. But the
revolting nature of the story, and the anti-climax of the
fifth act, in which the several villains kill one another,
are beyond the reach of the reformer's skill.
    For the style in which the piece is produced the mana-
gers and actors of Sadler's Wells are entitled to all
praise. Miss Glyn's performance of the Duchess is one of
the most striking achievements of that rising actress. The

scenes, intrinsically coarse, in which she makes love to
her steward, were admirably softened by the playful spirit
of coquetry which she infused into them. The soft passages of sorrow stole with mournful effect upon the naturally mirthful temperament, and when her wrongs aroused
her alike to a sense of pain and dignity, her denunciations
were terrific. Ferdinand is a less refined character than
the Duchess, but the transition from malice to remorse was
finely represented by Mr. Phelps, and Mr. G. Bennett is a
thorough intentional villain in the part of Bosola.

At the end the applause of the audience was loud, con-
tinuous, and unanimous, and Mr. Horne and all the chief
actors were called for.

(c) Sadler's Wells — 'The Duchess of Malfi,' altered by
Mr. R.H. Horne from old John Webster's celebrated tragedy,
was produced on Wednesday. This play, though written evidently in a religious spirit, lacks that fine humanity
which looks so beautiful in Shakespeare. Webster is a
gloomy believer in man's depravity, and seeks the tragic
in his crimes. We have here, indeed, the tragedy of the
churchyard; the fetid atmosphere of the charnel is that
breathed by the stern old poet. — The shade of the yew
darkens his pictures, and the shriek of the mandrake
maddens his scenes. Such are the usual images with which
the dialogue of Webster is burthened, — and the persons
of his dramas are fitted to these, both in their acts and
in their motives. The only exception in the present tragedy is, the character of the Duchess of Malfy herself; —
who, nevertheless, is affected by the evil of her position,
and made to seem criminal when indulging a virtuous passion. The Duchess of Malfi is the victim of a secret
marriage, and the mother of three children (in Mr. Horne's
version reduced to two), — whose fault of choosing beneath
her station is resented by a haughty brother, even to the
extent of the death of all parties concerned — excepting
one, a son of the unfortunate pair, who, in the original
play, survives the general ruin. Duke Ferdinand, the re-
vengeful brother, becomes a lycanthropist, as a fitting
consummation of his guilt. This part of the play is de-
cidedly the weakest: — though much benefited by Mr.
Horne's judicious alterations in the fifth act.

The Duke's agent, Bosola, is the strongest and most
efficient character. It was very properly confided to
Mr. G. Bennett, who performed it with great force, and
that old feeling for the histrionic art which few modern
professors seem to understand. Mr. Phelps struggled hard
to overcome the inherent difficulties of the part of

Ferdinand, — and to some extent succeeded. But no genius
could have achieved a triumph in such a part: — the utmost that talent, controlled by more than ordinary judgment
and taste, could effect, was to render it endurable. Some
startling stage effects, were, however, made. The mad
scenes were finely rendered. The nobleminded woman who
vainly endeavoured to plant the domestic affections in a
courtly soil, found a suitable representative in Miss Glyn.
Her usual originality of conception marked her performance
throughout. The character in her hands had two phases —
comic, and tragic. In the early scenes she was the lively
lady, loving and beloved; in the latter ones, she became
majestic, — a being to move terror and pity. Her last
scene, in which she suffers strangulation approaches to
the horrible in its details; but the art of the actress
was equal to the peril of the situation, and commanded
sympathy.

Mr. Horne has accomplished his stage adaptation of this
old drama with much tact and talent: — no pains, however,
can wholly get rid of its original clumsy structure.
Nothing is more conducive to a right estimate of Shakespeare's art than the contrast in regard to construction
which dramas of this class present with the most careless
of his. Compared with 'Othello' and 'The Tempest,' they
offer masses of modern extravagance. — We cannot say that
experiments like the present are to be commended. While
Webster is wholly unfitted to the modern stage, — we have
here not even Webster. But for the purpose of restoring
one of our old dramatists, there is no argument for this
reproduction, — and the alterations made to render the
reproduction possible, prove that he cannot be restored.

The costumes and scenery were costly and picturesque,
and the *mise en scene* displayed admirable tact and invention. This must be carried to the account of Mr. Phelps,
as stage manager, — to whose intelligence it is understood that such arrangements at this theatre are always
due. The house was crowded. Though evidently somewhat
puzzled by the horror of the situation, the beauties of
the dialogue seemed to be appreciated by the pit: — and
at the conclusion the applause was loud. Miss Glyn, Mr.
Phelps, Mr. Bennett, and Mr. Horne were called to receive
the accustomed congratulations. A prologue written by
Mr. Horne and spoken by Mr. Hoskins, preceded the performance.

(d) The Elizabethan dramatist John Webster, whose works,
admirably edited by the Reverend Alexander Dyce, fill four
such respectable volumes, is one of those gentlemen who

have reaped the full benefit of a reaction. When he had
been all but forgotten for something like a century, those
literary critics to whom we are so much indebted for their
revival of a taste for the earlier English literature chose
John Webster as an especial theme for eulogy. The more
generally familiar Elizabethans, such as Jonson, Beaumont,
Fletcher, and Massinger, were less respectfully treated;
but the rude strength of Webster could hardly be praised
enough. Like many other reactions, this, in our opinion,
went too far, and an honour was paid to one of our least
polished poets scarcely less than what is rightfully
awarded to an Aeschylus.

The production of 'The Duchess of Malfi' at Sadler's
Wells brings this idol for the first time before a modern
public; and, like many other idols, he will gain little by
ocular inspection. As a whole the play is but a sorry
work, showing equally the strength and the untutored condition of the mind that produced it. The story, setting
forth the slow process by which two fiendish brothers murdered their sister, a regnant duchess, as a punishment for
a mésalliance, has in itself no further interest than may
be found in any atrocity of journalistic renown. The accumulated horrors of the fourth act, which give the play
its character, are followed by a fifth so feeble and ridi-
culously murderous, that nothing can exceed the anti-climax.
The personages, far from being psychologically elaborated,
are flung upon the stage as so many lumps of moral deformity. In the language there is not the elevation of Marlowe's
earliest plays, which even when they touch the ridiculous
are still replete with poetical sublimity; but on the contrary, ideality is shunned for the sake of realism in its
uncouthest form. What may be said of most poets of an untutored age applies to Webster in particular. In the 150
pages which his play occupies, passages of matchless force
(we will not say *beauty*) may be found; and these are the
more remarkable as they strike suddenly, and we feel ourselves unexpectedly moved after long tasting most unsavoury
fare.

Mr. R.H. Horne, who has achieved the task of making
'The Duchess of Malfi' endurable enough not to send an
audience rushing out of a house, by removing from Webster's
play those means of excitement which appeal less to the imagination than to the stomach, exhibits all that care which
attends a labour of love. He has rearranged and dovetailed
passages at an expense of toil which can have been scarcely
less than that of producing an original work. But after
all, might not his fine poetical mind have been better
employed than in making a rough-hewn work appear a degree
less rough-hewn? Would he not contribute more to the

elevation of the drama by looking over one of his own plays
with a view to scenic production? As for 'The Duchess of
Malfi' being taken as any model of theatrical composition,
it is totally out of the question. Placing it by the side
of another play which is based on the principle of terror,
can any impartial, *practical* judge, say that it approaches
an equality to that French banquet of atrocities the
'Lucréce Borgia' of Victor Hugo?

In the acting of the piece, the great feature is the
very excellent performance of Miss Glyn; and we would
especially commend her treatment of the earlier portion
of the drama. The forcible passages that afterwards occur
may be said, in a way, to act themselves; but the difficulties at starting required delicate discrimination. The
Duchess is made to avow her passion to her steward, with a
freedom that is almost repulsive, and might be rendered
exceedingly so by a coarse treatment. Miss Glyn, by giving
the love-scene the tone of haute comédie, veils the indeli-
cacy of the position by an air of polished badinage. This
treatment also secures the advantage of contrast for the
misery that follows, and relieves the general ghastliness
of the play.

(e) Among the pardonable errors of my youth, I count the
belief that our old English dramatists were worthy of study
as men of true dramatic genius. Pardonable, I say, because
I was lured into it by a reverential regard felt for Lamb,
Hazlitt, and others, as fine critics, and by the unmistakable beauties of the scenes and passages they quoted. My
days and nights were given to Marlowe, Dekker, Webster,
Marston, Kyd, Greene, Peele, and the illustrious obscure
in Dodsley. Enthusiasm, however, was tamed by the irre-
sistible mediocrity of these plays; no belief in their excellence could long stand up against the evidence of their
dreariness and foolishness. I underlined fine passages;
copied apophthegms and beauties into various notebooks;
wrote foolish articles in magazines expressive of my admiration: but the thing could not last, and I silently
gave up my former idols to the scorn of whoso pleased to
vilify them. Looking backwards to the days of Lamb —
especially bearing in mind his peculiar idiosyncrasies —
the admiration he felt, and tried to inspire others with,
is perfectly intelligible; but, as I said some months ago
in these columns, the resuscitation of those dramatists
has been a fatal obstruction to the progress of the drama,
and has misled many a brave and generous talent. It has
fostered the tendency and flattered the weakness of poets,
by encouraging them to believe that mere writing suffices

for a drama — that imagery will supply the place of incidents, and that tragic *intentions* which boldly appeal to the imagination, are enough.

Nothing was needed to burst this bubble but the actual revival of a play or two upon the modern stage. Marston's 'Malcontent' was rudely tried at the Olympic; and now 'The Duchess of Malfi,' by John Webster, the most admired of the company excepting Marlowe, has been elaborately prepared by R.H. Horne, and produced at Sadler's Wells with all the care and picturesqueness for which that theatre is known. I have read that play four times, but although Horne has greatly lessened its absurdities, I never felt them so vividly until it was acted before my eyes. He has made it less tedious and less childish in its horrors, but the irredeemable mediocrity of its *dramatic* evolution of human passion is unmistakable. The noble lines of manly verse which charm the *reader* fail to arrest the *spectator*, who is alternating between impressions of the wearisome and the ludicrous.

Consider it under what aspect you will, short of a commonplace book of 'passages,' 'The Duchess of Malfi' is a feeble and a foolish work. I say this fully aware of the authorities against me — fully aware of the 'passages' which may be quoted as specimen-bricks. Other critics have declaimed against its accumulation of horrors; to my mind that is not the greatest defect. Instead of 'holding the mirror up to nature,' this drama holds the mirror up to Madame Tussaud's and emulates her 'chamber of horrors' but the 'worst remains behind,' and that is the motiveless and false exhibition of human nature. Take the story. The young Duchess of Malfi loves her steward, tells him so, and privately marries him. Her brothers Ferdinand and the Cardinal, caring only for the nobility of their lineage, with to marry her to Prince Malateste; and, on hearing how she has disgraced herself, resolve to kill her. But death, simply as death, is no fit punishment for such a crime. They prepare, therefore, a waxen image (anticipating Madame Tussaud) of Antonio, her husband, which is shown to her as his corpse; they fill her palace with mad people, whose howlings are to madden her; and, having wrought upon her till they think despair can hold out no longer, they bring in the executioners and strangle her. No sooner is she dead than Ferdinand, who planned it all, turns suddenly remorseful — as villains do in the last scenes of melodramas — and in the fifth act he goes raving mad. Now, firstly, the horrors are childish, because they grow out of no proper ground. They are not the culmination of tragic motives. The insulated pride of Ferdinand might demand as reparation the life of his sister, and there is a real

tragic position in the third act, where he places the
poinard in her hand and bids her die.   But playing these
fantastic tricks to bring her to despair is mere madness.
How ludicrously absurd is this Ferdinand — who has never
given a hint of any love for his sister, any sorrow for
her shame, any reluctance in perpetrating these cruelties —
to be suddenly lachrymose and repentant as soon as she is
dead!   This is not the work of a *dramatist*;   it is clumsy
ignorance.   'The Duchess of Malfi' is a nightmare, not a
tragedy.

I might go through the work, and point out in almost
every scene evidences of a similar incapacity for high
dramatic art;   but to what purpose?   Every year plays are
published by misguided young gentlemen exhibiting this
kind of incapacity, and friendly critics have no greater
compliment than to declare that the 'mantle of the Elizabethan dramatists has fallen upon Mr. Jones.'   If
Shakespeare is a great dramatist, Webster and company are
not dramatists at all;   and nothing exalts him more than to
measure him by his contemporaries.

Despising probabilities, disregarding all conditions of
art, and falsifying human nature, 'The Duchess of Malfi' is,
nevertheless, an attractive play to that audience.   As a
terrific melodrame, it delights the pit.   It was, therefore,
not a bad speculation to produce this adaptation, which,
let me say once for all, must have cost Horne more labour
than he will gain credit for.   As a poet, Horne is known
to wield 'Marlowe's mighty line' like a kindred spirit.   In
these additions to Webster we defy the nicest critic to
detect the old from the new;   unless you have the two books
side by side, you cannot tell whether you are reading
Webster or Horne.   But he would write a better play himself, and his labour would better be employed.   Why waste
his faculties in the hopeless task of making falsehood
look like truth?   'Cosmo de Medici', impracticable though
it be, is worth any amount of Webster.

The acting of this play reflects credit on the theatre.
Miss Glyn was better than we have yet seen her;   but this
intelligent actress will never achieve the position she
aspires to, unless she make a radical change in her style,
and throw aside the affectations and conventions she has
acquired.   Her elocution is vicious.   She chaunts instead
of speaking, and her chaunt is unmusical.   Instead of taking the rhythm from the verse, the accent from the sense,
she puts one monotonous rhythm upon the verse, and lets
the accent obey the impetus of the chaunt, as if the voice
mastered her, instead of her mastering the voice.   Once
or twice when she spoke naturally it was quite charming;
and her grand burst of despair, in the fourth act, though

injured by defect of chaunting, had so much force and fury
in it that the house shook with plaudits.   The comedy of
the early scenes was hard, forced, and stagey.   In making
love to her steward she wanted tenderness, grace, and coy-
ness.   On the whole, however, one may say that, except
Helen Faucit, no English actress could have played the part
so well.   Phelps was ill at ease in the first four acts, as
if the nonsense of his part baffled him, and he could not
grasp it;   towards the close of the fourth act, however,
he made a clutch at it, and his madness in the fifth act
was terribly real.   George Bennett, in Bosola, was suited
to a nicety.

29.   ISABELLA GLYN TOURS AS THE DUCHESS

1852-68

_____

During the eighteen years Isabella Glyn starred as the
Duchess of Malfi, the reviewers, with a few exceptions,
praised her performance while often expressing some dis-
taste for the play itself.   Of interest is the playfulness
Miss Glyn, on occasion in her career an accomplished
comedienne, brought to the earlier scenes of the play,
thus contrasting with the tragic despair manifested in
the fourth act.   It is a coquetry not immediately seen in
Horne's pedestrian text;   for this audiences should have
been thankful.   We may note also the new 'effect' in 1855
in which the Duchess appeared as her ghost in a moonlit
echo scene, and the elaborate set noted for the scene of
the Duchess's capture: the open country at midnight, 'with
the moonlight reflected in the rippling waters of the lake'.
    Excerpts from (a) the 'Manchester Guardian', 23 October
1852, p. 8;   (b) 'The Times', London, 2 April 1855, p. 5;
(c)   the Dublin 'Daily Express', 25 November 1858, p. 3;
(d)   'The Times', London, 14 April 1868, p. 9.

_____

(a)   [The writer lengthily recounts the plot and quotes
and praises 'Shakespearian' passages.]

So far we have described the printed, and not the acted,
drama, which ends with the death of the duchess in the
fourth act.   It has, as it seems to say, great errors in

construction. It is unlikely that in her own territory,
a sovereign duchess should be seized, imprisoned in her
own palace, none of her greatest subjects permitted to
see her; the people, a mere shadowy myth, suffering her
to be cruelly done to death.... There seems no reason why
the duchess should for two years conceal her marriage,
even after the birth of her second child.... In short,
the dramatist, in effect, begs the auditor and reader to
concede to him that his virtuous and high-minded couple
are weak, timid, trembling creatures, who dare not avow
their union before the world.... It has also much more
clap-trap, stage trickery, as for instance, making Bosola
disguise himself as an old man.... The joyous nature of
Marina is finely displayed by [Miss Glyn] in the badinage
with her husband in the chamber; her dignity and self-
possession in the interview which immediately follows with
Ferdinand, and which only makes it the more difficult to
realize her subsequent shrinking and apprehension. Nervous in her terrors, the moment real danger arrives, she
reasserts the constancy of her soul, and defies it. But
she yields passively to this tyranny from which one vigorous assertion of her rights would have freed her; and it
is this fatal inconsistency in the character, as drawn by
the dramatist, which prevents Miss Glyn from achieving any
great triumph in the part.... Mr. Swinbourn (Ferdinand),
in aiming to display the raving of disappointed rage, burst
out into a rant which provoked laughter.... On the whole,
we cannot think this old play a happy revival, though it is
wholly free from grossness.

(b)   ...Altogether, we strongly suspect that the neighbors
of the Eastern Countries Terminus prefer John Webster to
William Shakespeare — that is to say, as typified in the
two plays of 'The Duchess of Malfi' and 'Antony and Cleopatra'. The latter work presupposes something like a
knowledge of history, which one may not always have con-
veniently at hand; but the former, the creation of old,
terrible Webster, is made up of a mass of horrors, which,
though they nominally occur in Amalfi (or, as honest John
calls it, 'Malfi'), are intelligible to those who are
blessed with no more learning as to the doings of mankind
than can be obtained from the reports of the Central Criminal Court. Moreover, the horrors are good, substantial
horrors....
    Miss Glyn's interpretation of the Duchess, which con-
sists in giving a comic tone to the earlier scenes and
idealizing as much as possible the circumstances of the
dreadful death, so as to at once avoid coarseness and to

produce a strong contrast, is already familiar; indeed it
is she alone who has preserved the vitality of the play....
Nor should we forget the new 'effect' in the scene where the
echo from the tomb summons the bereaved Antonio. Formerly
the wailing voice belonged to the prompter, but now Miss
Glyn answers *in propria persona*, and then glides away as
the ghost of herself in a style worthy of a Corsican-
brother.

(c) The 'Duchess of Malfi,' a tragedy adapted from the
origins of John Webster, a noted playwright of the Beaumont
and Fletcher era, was produced for the first time in Dublin
at the Theatre Royal on Tuesday night. This drama had remained in complete oblivion — so far as its non-production
on the stage could be so considered — from the time of its
first representation at the Blackfriars Theatre in 1640,
until 1850, when it was revived by Mr. Phelps at Sadler's
Wells, the part of the Duchess being then sustained by Miss
Glyn. Her impersonation of the character was so vivid and
impressive as to achieve for the piece a success which might
in some degree be considered a compensation for the neglect
to which it had been so long consigned, and which, to any
mere reader of the play (with all due respect to the memory
of 'Old John Webster') must have seemed extraordinary, were
not the wonders within the scope of histrionic genius reflected upon. In point of poetic thought and expression
this tragedy appears very defective indeed, when contrasted
with the master-pieces of some of the writer's contemporaries; but it nevertheless possesses that one merit which
in all cases seems sufficient to insure for any stage composition a respectable vitality — namely a well-defined
and startling plot, in which the tragic element is sustained
and developed with increasing power to the climax, which
culminates in four several murders. The story is briefly
as follows: — The Duchess of Malfi, a young and beautiful
widow, falls in love with and secretly marries her steward,
Antonio Bologna. Her brothers, the Duke Ferdinand and the
Prince Graziani, are desirous that she should form an
alliance with the noble Prince Malateste, who is a suitor
for her hand, and, with the view of being informed as to
her private movements, they induce her to hire as her master of horse one Bossola, a man of desperate fortune, who
is a spy in their service. After an interval, this man
becomes aware of the nature of the relations existing between the Duchess and Antonio, and communicates the fact to
the brothers, who are enraged at what they conceive to be
the dishonour entailed upon their noble house, in the marriage of their sister with a man of such obscure position.

The Duke flies to Malfi, and imprisons the Duchess in her
palace, Antonio having just before Ferdinand's arrival
escaped with his children to Ancona, whither his wife had
arranged to follow him. Bossola is then induced by the
brothers, on condition that the title of Count shall be
conferred upon him, to secretly strangle the Duchess, the
perpetration of which crime is followed by the remorse of
the Duke, who, in a frenzy, threatens to deliver up Bossola as a murderer. The latter then determines upon the
death of the Duke, and on a certain dark night falls upon
and kills a man whom he mistakes for his intended victim,
but who turns out to be no other than Antonio returned
from Ancona in search of his wife. At this juncture the
Duke enters in a wild and excited mood, followed by his
brother, whom he taunts with having been the instigator
of the foul murder of their sister, and then rushes upon
and slays. Bossola and he then meet, mutually attack, and
kill each other, whereupon, after a dying speech or two,
the curtain drops.
     In the character of the Duchess, Miss Glyn had ample
range for the display of her versatile genius, — the
scene in which she acknowledges her love to Antonio, and
expresses her wish to become his wife, being acted with a
grace and vivacity quite charming; whilst in the subsequent tragic passages she evinced a pathos and energy which
might bear comparison with the highest efforts of any tra-
gedienne of our day. Mr. Montgomery — who is seen with
increased advantage on each successive appearance — represented the part of the Duke with consummate ability, avoid-
ing the slightest approach to exaggeration either of de-
clamation or gesture, whilst preserving all the force and
spirit essential to an adequate rendering of the part.
Miss Glyn and Mr. Montgomery were both called before the
curtain on the conclusion of the piece.
     The play was repeated last night to a good house. The
comic drama, 'The Two Queens,' concluded the entertainment.

(d) [The writer appreciates the managerial effort to
bring a 'higher and more legitimate class of entertainment'
to the new theatre in Shoreditch, but admits that 'the
production of a play like "The Duchess of Malfi" is, to
say the least, a hazardous experiment'. He recounts Webster's biography, his sources, the stage history of the
play, concluding: 'It is impossible that Webster's "Duchess
of Malfi", even with its more repellent prominences softened
down in Mr. Horne's version, can ever retain a permanent
hold on the stage. Like Joanna Baillie's "De Montfort", it
is a fine poem but an accumulation of horrors — an unmiti-

gated display of the terrible graces.' Though much has
been done, notes the critic, to secure a favourable response to the play, the efforts, except for Miss Glyn's
performance, are 'of no avail'.]

It would be impossible to speak too highly of Miss Glyn's
impersonation of the Duchess. Her name is exclusively
associated with the character, for, to use an Italian
phrase, she has never been 'doubled' in it. Replete with
all the varieties of depth and solemn brilliancy, her performance comprehends everything that could be wished for....
The most remarkable individual beauties in her performance
were her delivery of those exquisitely poetical lines —

    The birds that live i' th' field
    On the wild benefit of nature, live
    Happier than we; for they may choose their mates,
    And carol their sweet pleasures to the spring,

in which her tone and manner lent double grace and beauty
to the image; and in that passage when, in reply to
Bosola's taunts as to her misery and degradation, she collected up all her dignity and pride to bid him remember
that she was 'Duchess of Malfi still'.... The piece was
admirably put upon the stage, and one of the scenes — a
view of the open country at midnight, with the moonlight
reflected in the rippling waters of a lake — was very
beautiful.

30. 'THE DUCHESS' IN THE USA

1857-9

On 22 August 1857, 'The Duchess of Malfi' was introduced
to the USA at the American Theatre in San Francisco. James
Stark, the actor-manager who directed his wife Sarah in
the title role with himself as Ferdinand, greatly revised
Horne's fifth act and included even more settings and
effects. His most triumphant addition came at the close
of the play: an 'apotheosis' tableau of the Duchess and
Antonio sentimentally reunited in death, amid clouds and
'blue fire when cloud ascends'. Yet it was the Wilmarth
Wallers who soon achieved the greatest successes with the
play in the USA. Waller, an American actor who played

Antonio in the original Sadler's Wells revival, directed
his wife Emma and, like Stark, portrayed Ferdinand.
Although receiving mixed reviews on her first attempts
at the Duchess, Mrs Waller went on to rival Isabella Glyn's
success, playing the role for the next twenty-five years.
Perhaps even more than the Starks, the Wallers sensation-
alized Horne's text, as the Philadelphia review indicates:
at the close, the Duchess was seen 'riding to heaven, in
white muslin'. Frank W. Wadsworth, in his helpful study,
American Performances of the 'Duchess of Malfi', in
'Theatre Survey', II (1970), pp. 151-66, examines the ex-
tant prompt-books and conjectures that these closing tableaux represented a strange marriage between Webster and
Harriet Beecher Stowe: audiences had thrilled to George
Aiken's stage adaptation of 'Uncle Tom's Cabin' since
1852, with its climactic tableau wherein Little Eva was
'discovered' on the back of a milk-white dove, presumably
en route to heaven. Sentimental moral victories were thus
achieved in both plays, delighting the audiences but, as
so often in the case of Webster, not always the reviewers.
    Excerpts from (a) the New Orleans 'Daily Picayune', 11
December 1857, p. 5; (b) the 'New York Times', 7 April
1858, p. 4; (c) the 'Spirit of the Times', 10 April 1858,
p. 108; (d) the 'New York Daily Tribune', 6 April 1858,
p. 5; (e) the 'New York Herald', 6 April 1858, p. 7;
(f) the 'Philadelphia Press', 26 April 1859, p. 2.

(a) There was a good house at the St. Charles theatre last
evening, to witness the first performance, in this city,
of the tragedy called 'The Duchess of Malfi,' which was
written by John Webster, 'the noble minded,' as Hazlitt
designates him, who lived and wrote in the first half of
the seventeenth century. He died about the year 1640, and
the best critics have awarded him a high rank among the
dramatists that have left their work upon English literature....
    The plot of this deep tragedy turns on the mortal offence
which Marina, the Duchess of Malfi (Mrs. Stark) gives to her
two proud brothers, Duke Ferdinand (Mr. Stark) and the Cardinal Graziana (Mr. Swan), by indulging in a generous
though infatuated passion for Antonio (Mr. Wright), a gentleman of her court, and whom she privately marries.

[The critic praises Mrs Stark's portrayal in the wooing
scene, with its 'exquisite touches of feeling'. It is the
scene 'which above most of them will be remembered with
pleasure'. The plot is recounted, and the death of the

Duchess is described, 'a hideous refinement of cruelty'.
The writer quotes briefly from the Duchess's last
speeches.]

    She is led out by the masks [masked attendants], with
the cord placed by her own hands about her neck;   a stifled
scream is heard, and the Duchess staggers in, and falls dead
upon the stage.   Ferdinand enters and is struck with remorse
at the sight of his twin sister lying there a corpse, the
victim of his own terrible revenge.   The woe he sought but
vainly to inflict on her becomes his own, and he goes distraught....
    Full as this play is of highly dramatic situations, ad-
mirably drawn and naturally colored as are all the characters, and abounding as it certainly is with eloquent and
powerful language, we confess that it is too highly
wrought with what the biographer of Webster designates as
'supernumerary horrors,' to suit our taste as an acting
play;   and we should be quite resigned to its speedy return to the shelves of the library, from which we do not
think it will prove a successful experiment to have taken
it down. It is true that we are invited to 'sup full of
horrors,' over such banquets as Shakespeare, and Otway,
and Congreve, and Rowe, and others of the standard dramatists have provided in plentiful profusion for us.   But
let us rest content with the bowl of the Borgia, the cord
of poor Cordelia, the envenomed steel of Hamlet, without
seeking to add to the terrible list forgotten horrors;
presented to us as though they may be in forms of classic
grace and made seductive by words instinct with genius.
    'The Duchess of Malfi' is to be repeated this evening,
and only on this single occasion.   It is very forcibly
and impressively performed, every character in it well
sustained;   and to those who are fond of the manifesta-
tion and development of the tragic element in its fullest
intensity, will prove a not unacceptable performance.

(b)   Broadway Theatre — To the explorer of ancient dramatic literature, John Webster's play of the 'Duchess of
Malfi' comes like a flash of light.   Not that its merits
in themselves are especially brilliant, but because they
contrast favorably with the feeble glimmers emitted by
some others of Shakespeare's contemporaries.   The tragedy
is of the thrilling kind, and abounds in horrible situations, whilst the plot is blood-thirsty to the last degree.   The dialogue is pompous without always being elevated, but at times it touches the poetic standard and is
grand.   As an acting play, the version given by Mr. and

Mrs. Waller last evening at the Broadway, has everything
to recommend it, and even those faults which are un-
palatable to the student are not unwelcome to an audience.
   Mrs. Waller is a lady of decided talent, although a
little wild and restless, and also a little conventional.
She aims largely for effects, and wins them generally in
the old-fashioned way, but sometimes she permits her native
talent to have full sway, and then something more brilliant
than common tragic tinsel is the result. A few performances before a Metropolitan audience will, we trust, place
this lady in a favorable light with the public. We were
unable to detect any particular merit in Mr. Waller beyond that which belongs to any stock actor.
   The tragedy is well played, and has been put on the
stage in a careful manner.

(c) ...Mr. and Mrs. Waller are certainly clever artists,
but both possess the same fault — a grievous one in a
New York theatre — that of *ranting*: they are too stagey,
and pay too little regard to nature. Mrs. Waller has a
fine figure, a very pleasing countenance, and a sweet
voice, all of which she manages well in the quiet scenes,
looking every inch a Duchess and a pretty young widow.
Mr. Waller's Ferdinand was altogether too boisterous as
we have intimated above, but he has in him the stuff for
a first-class actor, and we doubt not he will profit by
the advice which he will receive.... The tragedy itself
is of the most gloomy and unnatural description. Some
horrid noises in the fourth act, which caused considerable
merriment when the author intended everybody to cry, somewhat relieved the general monotony; but we would rather
at that time have sympathized with the unfortunate Duchess
and watched intently the emotions of Mrs. Waller, than to
have been distracted by inquiries in audible whispers as
to whether the elephant had been removed, with a general
tittering throughout the house.

(d) John Webster's play, 'The Duchess of Malfi,' was performed last night, introducing to the audience Mr. and Mrs.
Waller. The merits of this old drama may be summed up in
saying that it has occasionally some very strong lines.
The plot is not good, and the situations are spasmodically
forced up to tragedy, without the self-working which distinguishes a first class work of art; besides, it is an
essentially meager and disagreeable story as a whole. A
proud and cruel ducal brother torturing and killing a
widowed Duchess, because she was secretly married to a

gentleman of inferior rank, but of good repute, seems to
us poor stuff for five acts of somberness, hardly relieved
by a touch of every-day emotion and sentiment....
    We feel bound to add that the audience applauded heart-
ily, and called Mr. and Mrs. Waller before the curtain;
and if they are satisfied, so it may be said should be the
critics. The play was well put on the stage; and excepting the awful tragic noises behind the scenes in the fourth
act, kept the audience as serious as could be wished.
These, though set down in the book, made the listeners
laugh during the death scenes of the Duchess. On the repe-
tition of the drama, a little modification at this point
would be well.

(e) Mr. and Mrs. Waller made their first appearance at
the Broadway last night in the old Elizabethan five-act
tragedy of John Webster, a contemporary of the immortal
Will Shakespeare, the 'Duchess of Malfi'. The old play
has been considerably modernized, and in some instances
not with much advantage. For example, the attempt to
dovetail the illegitimate into the legitimate drama by
the introduction of tableaux and sensation scenes, though
perhaps in accordance with the prevailing taste of the day,
was not to our mind quite successful, nor in keeping with
the spirit of the author. However, that may be, it is
certain that the play had a brilliant success last night,
and is destined to enjoy a long run.... The house was well-
filled, and the greatest enthusiasm was evinced throughout
the entire performance. In modernising the rendering of
the 'Duchess of Malfi', however, we think that more ingenuity might have been displayed in the fifth act. In the
present representation all the villains, but whom it seemed
essential to kill off in order to perfect the tragic character of the play, are dispatched in a heap, and with a
celerity which is somewhat disagreeable to witness. In
truth, the play would end better with the fourth than the
fifth act, with a little amendment in the plot: the impressions of both of the drama and the actors would be far
more pleasurable....

(f) A large audience, at Walnut-street Theatre, gave a
hearty salutation to Mr. and Mrs. Waller.... The play was
Webster's 'Duchess of Malfi', adapted to the sense of propriety which audiences of the present day feel more delicately than our forefathers did, in the early days of the
drama....

There is a scene of novel power, in which Antonio,
ignorant of his wife's death, has responses of his own
words made to him by an echo from his grave. Next time,
Echo must raise her voice. Bosola, repentant, seeks to
save Antonio's life, but accidentally slays him in the
dark, and is threatening the Cardinal, when the Duke, mad
with remorse and rage, kills both, receiving his own
death-stab from Bosola. The curtain falls on the four
dead men, and an allegorical tableau follows.
    Mrs. Waller played the Duchess about as ably as it could
be played. The most exquisite scene was that in which she
woos Antonio, without overstepping the modesty of her sex.
Mr. Waller scarcely pleased us until after the death of
the Duchess, when his rage became subdued by remorse....
    The play was well placed in the stage, and the dresses
good — those of the Wallers splendid — except the Cardinal's miserable apology for sacerdotal vestments. The
echoes in the fifth act were scarcely audible in front,
and the scene showing the Duchess riding to Heaven, in
white muslin, was a needless interpolation.... Neither,
when the play was ended did we like the pause necessary to
show a sort of apotheosis of the Duchess.
    Mrs. Waller was called for at the end of acts III and
IV, and, with Mr. Waller, again at the end of the play.

31. THE CANON FIRES

1856

Extracts from 'Plays and Puritans' by Charles Kingsley
(1819-75), novelist, social reformer, and canon of West-
minster. As a Victorian moralist, Kingsley naturally
wanted 'truth' and 'living persons' in plays which should
uplift the masses. His powerful attack marks the opening
of the debate over Webster's moral view, an argument which
continued into the twentieth century. Extracts from the
1885 edition, pp. 18, 50-6. Originally published in the
'North British Review', 1856.

The whole story of 'Vittoria Corombona' is one of sin and
horror. The subject-matter of the play is altogether made
up of the fiercest and basest passions. But the play is

not a study of those passions from which we may gain a
great insight into human nature.   There is no trace —
nor is there, again, in the 'Duchess of Malfi' — of that
development of human souls for good or evil which is
Shakespeare's especial power — the power which, far more
than any accidental 'beauties,' makes his plays to this
day, the delight alike of the simple and the wise, while
his contemporaries are all but forgotten. The highest
aim of dramatic art is to exhibit the development of the
human soul, to construct dramas in which the conclusion
shall depend, not on the events, but on the characters;
and in which the characters shall not be mere embodiments
of a certain passion, or a certain 'humour': but persons,
each unlike all. Thus, each having a destiny of his own
peculiarities, and of his own will.... This is indeed 'high
art': but we find no more of it in Webster than in the
rest. His characters, be they young or old, come on the
stage ready-made, full grown, and stereotyped; and therefore, in general, they are not characters at all, but mere
passions or humours in human form. Now and then he essays
to draw a character: but it is analytically, by description,
not synthetically and dramatically, but letting the man exhibit himself in action; and in the 'Duchess of Malfi', he
falls into the great mistake of telling, by Antonio's
mouth, more about the Duke and Cardinal than he afterwards
makes them act....
     But the truth is, the study of human nature is not Web-
ster's aim. He has to arouse terror and pity, not thought,
and he does it in his own way, by blood and fury, madmen
and screech-owls, not without a rugged power. There are
scenes of his, certainly, like that of Vittoria's trial,
which have been praised for their delineation of character:
but it is one thing to solve the problem, which Shakespeare
has so handled in 'Lear', 'Othello', and 'Richard the Third' —
'Given a mixed character, to show how he may become criminal';
and to solve Webster's — 'Given a ready-made criminal, to
show how he commits his crimes.' To us the knowledge of
character shown in Vittoria's trial scene is not an insight
into Vittoria's essential heart and brain, but a general
acquaintance with the conduct of all bold bad women when
brought to bay ... the strength of Webster's confest master
scene lies simply in intimate acquaintance with vicious
nature in general....
     The 'Duchess of Malfi' is certainly in a purer and lof-
tier strain, but in spite of the praise that has been
lavished on her, we must take the liberty to doubt whether
the poor Duchess is a 'person' at all. General goodness
and beauty, intense though pure affection for a man below
her in rank, and a will to carry out her purpose at all

hazards, are not enough to distinguish her from thousands
of other women: but Webster has no such purpose.   What
he was thinking of was not truth, but effect;   not the
Duchess, but her story;   not Antonio, her major-domo and
husband, but his good and bad fortunes;   and thus he has
made Antonio merely insipid, the brothers merely unnatural,
and the Duchess (in the critical moment of the play) merely
forward.   That curious scene, in which she acquaints Antonio with her love for him and makes him marry her, is, on
the whole, painful.   Webster himself seems to have felt that
it was so;   and, dreading lest he had gone too far, to have
tried to redeem the Duchess at the end by making her break
down in two exquisite lines of loving shame: but he has
utterly forgotten to explain or justify her love by giving
to Antonio (as Shakespeare would probably have done) such
strong specialties of character as would compel, and therefore excuse, his mistress' affection....   The prison scenes
between the Duchess and her tormentors are painful enough,
if to give pain be a dramatic virtue;   and she appears in
them really noble;   and might have appeared far more so,
had Webster taken half as much pains with her as he has
with the madmen, ruffians, ghosts, and screech owls in
which his heart really delights.   The only character
really worked out so as to live and grow under his hand is
Bosola, who, of course, is the villain of the piece, and
being a rough fabric, is easily manufactured with rough
tools.   Still Webster has his wonderful touches here and
there —

Cariola.   Hence, villains, tyrants, murderers! Alas!
           What will you do with my lady? Call for help!

Duchess.   To whom? to our next neighbors? they are mad folk.
           Farewell, Cariola.
           I pray thee look thou giv'st my little boy
           Some syrup for his cold; and let the girl
           Say her prayers ere she sleep. — Now, what you
               please;
           What death?

    And so the play ends, as does 'Vittoria Corrombona,'
with half a dozen murders *coram populo*, howls, despair,
bedlam, and the shambles....

32.   WEBSTER ON THE AMERICAN LECTURE CIRCUIT

1859

Edwin P. Whipple (1819-86), essayist and popular lecturer
in Boston and New York literary circles, notes Webster's
'steadiness of nerve and clearness of vision' in a lecture
given at the Lowell Institute, later published in 'The
Literature of the Age of Elizabeth' (1869), pp. 139-47.

Webster was one of those writers whose genius consists in
the expression of special moods, and who, outside of those
moods, cannot force their creative faculties into vigorous
action. His mind by instinctive sentiment was directed to
the contemplation of the darker aspects of life. He brooded
over crime and misery until his imagination was enveloped
in their atmosphere, found a fearful joy in probing their
sources and tracing their consequences, became strangely
familiar with their physiognomy and psychology, and felt a
shuddering sympathy with their 'deep groans and terrible
ghastly looks.' There was hardly a remote corner of the
soul, which hid a feeling capable of giving mental pain,
into which this artist in agony had not curiously peered;
and his meditations on the mysterious disorder produced
in the human consciousness by the rebound of thoughtless
or criminal deeds might have found fit expression in the
lines of a great poet of our own times: —

                    Action is momentary, ——
        The motion of a muscle, this way or that.
        Suffering is long, obscure, and infinite.

With this proclivity of his imagination, Webster's power
as a dramatist consists in confining the domain of his tragedy within definite limits, in excluding all variety of
incident and character which could interfere with his main
design of awakening terror and pity, and in the intensity
with which he arrests, and the tenacity with which he holds
the attention, as he drags the mind along the pathway which
begins in misfortune or guilt, and ends in death. He is
such a spendthrift of his stimulants, and accumulates horror
on horror, and crime on crime, with such fatal facility,
that he would render the mind callous to his terrors, were
it not that what is acted is still less than what is suggested, and that the souls of his characters are greater

than their suffering, or more terrible than their deeds.
The crimes and the criminals belong to Italy as it was in
the sixteenth century, when poisoning and assassination
were almost in the fashion; the feelings with which they
are regarded are English; and the result of the combination is to make the poisoners and assassins more fiend-
ishly malignant in spirit than they actually were. Thus
Ferdinand, in the 'Duchess of Malfy,' is the conception
formed by an honest, deep-thoughted Englishman of an
Italian duke and politician, who had been educated in
those maxims of policy which were generalized by Machia-
velli. Webster makes him a devil, but a devil with a soul
to be damned....
    We have said that Webster's peculiarity is the tenacity
of his hold on the mental and moral constitution of his
characters. We know of their appetites and passions and
by the effects of these on their souls. He has properly
no sensuousness. Thus in 'The White Devil,' his other
great tragedy, the events proceed from the passion of
Brachiano for Vittoria Corombona, — a passion so in-ense
as to lead one to order the murder of her husband. If
either Fletcher or Ford had attempted the subject, the
sensual and emotional motives to the crime would have been
represented with overpowering force, and expressed in the
most alluring images, so that wickedness would have been
almost resolved into weakness; but Webster lifts the
wickedness at once from the region of the senses into the
region of the soul, exhibits its results in sensual depravity, and shows the satanic energy of purpose which may
spring from the ruins of the moral will. There is nothing
lovable in Vittoria; she seems indeed, almost without
sensations; and the affection between her and Brachiano
is simply the magnetic attraction which one evil spirit
has for another evil spirit. Francisco, the brother of
Brachiano's wife, says to him: —

    'Thou has a wife, our sister; would I had given
    Both her white hands to death, bound and locked fast
    In her last winding-sheet, when I gave thee
    But one.'

    This is the language of the intensest passion, but as
applied to the adulterous lover of Victoria it seems little
more than the utterance of reasonable regret; for devil
only can truly mate with devil, and Vittoria is Brachiano's
real 'affinity.'
    The moral confusion they produce by their deeds is
treated with more than Webster's usual steadiness of nerve
and clearness of vision. The evil they inflict is a cause

of evil in others; the passion which leads to murder
rouses the fiercer passion which aches for vengeance; and
at last, when the avengers of crime have become morally as
bad as the criminals, they are all involved in a common
destruction. Vittoria is probably Webster's most powerful
delineation. Bold, bad, proud, glittering in her baleful
beauty, strong in that evil courage which shrinks from
crime as little as from danger, she meets her murderers
with the same self-reliant scorn with which she met her
judges....
    Of all the contemporaries of Shakespeare, Webster is
the most Shakespearian. His genius was not only influenced by its contact with one side of Shakespeare's many-
sided mind, but the tragedies we have been considering
abound in expressions and situations either suggested by
or directly copied from the tragedies of him he took for
his model....

33. J.A. SYMONDS IN THE 'CORNHILL MAGAZINE'

1865

Known in his own day as the historian of the Italian
Renaissance, John Addington Symonds (1940-93) would later
write the introduction to the Mermaid edition of Webster
and Tourneur (1888). As his seven volume 'Renaissance in
Italy' (1875-86) is marked by the fluent as well as the
florid, so is this earlier appreciation of Webster and his
colleagues. From The English Drama during the Reigns of
Elizabeth and James, 'Cornhill Magazine', XI (May 1965),
pp. 604-18.

At all periods of history the stage has been the mirror of
the spirit of the century in which it has arisen. Dramatic
poets give form to the ideas of their age, exhibiting its
common aims and hopes and wishes on a more magnificent
scale than that of daily life. To interpret men to themselves, to express in words what the majority can only
feel, and to leave in art a record of past ages to posterity,
is the function of all genius, but more especially of the
dramatic genius, which rules for its domain the passions and
manners of men. But while the stage thus sums up the

character of epochs in history, it never ceases to be
national.... Never since the birth of art in Greece has
any nation displayed a dramatic genius so spontaneous and
powerful [as England's], so thoroughly belonging to the
century in which it sprang, and so national in form and
spirit. Yet at the same time it is universal by right of
its commanding interest, of its insight into nature, of
its freedom from any prejudice, of its sympathy with every
phase of human feeling, of its meditation upon all the
problems that have vexed the world, of its accumulated
learning, of its vast experiences, and of the liberality
with which its wealth was cast unreckoned on the world....
    Yet in whatever scene [the playwrights] fixed the action
of their plays, we find the same exuberance of life and the
same vehement passions. In their delineation of character
there is no feebleness of execution. In their plots we
trace no lack of incidents, no languor of development.
Their art suffered rather from rapidity, excess of vigour,
and extravagant invention. To represent exciting scenes
by energetic action, to clothe audacious ideas in grandi-
loquent language, to imitate the broader aspects of passion, to quicken the dullest apprehensions by strong contrasts and 'sensational' effects, was the aim which authors
and actors pursued in common.... The Flamineo and Bosola
of Webster are the villains of a darker dye, men such as
only Italy of the sixteenth century could breed, courtiers
refined in arts of wickedness; subtle, polite, and
finished scholars; brave in war and bold in love; and
then, in ill repute and want of money, place themselves at
the command of princes to subserve their pleasures and
accomplish their revenge. In such men there is no faith,
no hope, and no remorse. Some devil seems to have sat for
their portraits.
    Insanity in [the dramatists'] hands became a powerful
instrument of moving pity and inspiring dread. There is
nothing more solemn than the consciousness of vacillating
reason which the Duchess of Malfi displays after she has
been confined in prison among lunatics and murderers. The
persecutors seek to drive her into madness. She argues
with herself whether she be mad or not.

[Quotes 'O that it were possible' and 'And custom makes it
easy'.]

    Extravagant passion, the love of love, or the hate of
hate, makes men tremble on the verge of insanity. This
state of exaltation, in which the whole nature quivers
beneath the shock of one overpowering desire, was admirably
revealed by the dramatists. Ferdinand, in Webster, kills

his sister from excess of jealousy and avarice. But when
he sees her corpse, his fancy, set on flame already by
the fury of his hate, becomes a kind of hell, which plagues
him always with the memory of her calm, pale face, fixed
eyes, and tender age....
   If the evil of the world was painted simply as it is in
all its strength and ugliness by our old dramatists, the
beauty and the peace, the loveliness of nature and the
dignity of soul which makes our life worth living, were
no less faithfully portrayed. The multiform existence we
enjoy upon this earth received a true reflection in our
theatre — nor was one aspect of its development neglected
for another. Those artists verily believed that 'the
world's a stage': they made their art a microcosm of the
universe.

34. WILLIAM MINTO ON WEBSTER AS DRAMATIST

1874

William Minto, Professor of English Literature at the University of Aberdeen, argues briefly for Webster as effective playwright, a somewhat singular approach among Victorian admirers of Webster. From his 'Characteristics of
English Poets', the American edition of 1897, p. 355.

And these plays are not merely closet-plays, whose excel-
lences can be picked out and admired only at leisure. The
characters have not the simplicity and popular intelligi-
bility of Shakespeare's Richard or Iago. The plots, too,
except in 'Appius and Virginia,' where all the incidents
lie in the direct line of the catastrophe, are involved with
obscure windings and turnings. Yet all the scenes are care-
fully constructed for dramatic effect. Mark how studious
Webster has been that his actors shall never go lamely off
the stage: they make their exit at happily chosen moments,
and with some remark calculated to leave a buzz of interest
behind them. When we look closely into Webster's plays we
become aware that no dramatist loses more in closet perusal:
all his dialogues were written with a careful eye to the
stage. Everywhere throughout his plays we meet with marks
of deep meditation and just design. It is not with his

plays as with Fletcher's. The more we study Webster, the
more we find to admire. His characters approach nearer to
the many-sidedness of real men and women than those of any
dramatist except Shakespeare; and his exhibition of the
changes of feeling wrought in them by the changing progress of events, though characterised by less of revealing
instinct and more of penetrating effort than appear in
Shakespeare, is hardly less powerful and true.

35. WARD'S 'HISTORY'

1875

A.W. Ward (1837-1924), historian, critic, and co-editor of
the 'Cambridge History of English Literature', provided
the first 'modern' history of the English drama with his
1875 'History of English Dramatic Literature'. Something
of a Victorian moralist, Ward denies Webster a moral and
tragic vision. From the second edition (1899), III, pp.
57-66.

     Ward considers first 'The White Devil', disagreeing
with Lamb and Dyce on the character of Vittoria: she is
a 'defiant sinner'. There are wonderful touches, but on
the whole 'we crave — and crave in vain — some relief to
the almost sickening combination of awe and loathing
created by such characters and motives as this drama presents'. 'The Duchess of Malfi' is, however, a 'masterly'
work, with 'flashes of genius which seem to light up of a
sudden a wide horizon of emotions'.

This extraordinary tragedy ['The White Devil'], whose finest
scenes and passages have, in the judgment of Mr. Swinburne,
been never surpassed or equalled except by Shakspere 'in
the crowning qualities of tragic or dramatic poetry,' must
be described as at once highly elaborated and essentially
imperfect. In the address *To the Reader* already referred
to, Webster confesses with conscious pride that this play
was the fruit of protracted labour; but his efforts
appear to have been directed rather to accumulating and
elaborating effective touches of detail than to producing
a well-proportioned whole. The catastrophe seems to lag
too far after the climax; and in spite of the mighty

impression created by the genius of the author, it is
difficult to resist a sense of weariness in the progress
of the later part of the action. But a yet more serious
defect appears to me to attach to 'Vittoria Corombona.'
The personages of this tragedy — above all that of the
heroine — are conceived with the most striking original
power and carried out with unerring consistency; but we
crave — and crave in vain — some relief to the almost
sickening combination of awe and loathing created by such
characters and motives as this drama presents.

The character of Vittoria herself — the White Devil —
this is a conception which we instinctively feel to be
true to nature — to nature, that is, in one of her abnormal moods. In the first scene in which Vittoria appears
she reveals the deadliness of her passionate resolution,
when relating to her paramour the dream which is to urge
him on to the murder of his duchess and her own husband.
The ghastliness of the imagery of the vision is indescrib-
ably effective, together with the horrible scornfulness of
the closing phrase:

When to my rescue there arose, methought,
A whirlwind, which let fall a massy arm
From that strong plant;
And both were struck dead by that sacred yew,
In that base shallow grave that was their due.

The scene in which Vittoria is tried for the murder of
her husband has attracted the comment of several critics —
among others of Charles Lamb, who strangely enough speaks
of her 'innocence-resembling boldness.' Dyce demurs to
this view, which appears to me utterly erroneous, and
destructive of the consistency which the character
throughout maintains. Not 'sweetness' and 'loveliness'
but a species of strange fascination, such as is only too
often exercised by heartless pride, seems to pervade the
figure and the speech of the defiant sinner who refuses
to withdraw an inch from the position which she has as-
sumed, and meets her judges with a front of withering
scorn. Almost equally effective are the burst of passion
with which she turns upon the jealous Brachiano, and the
gradual subsiding of her wrath, as of a fire, under his
caresses. The terrible energy of the last act is almost
unparalleled; but the character of Vittoria remains true
to itself, except perhaps in the last — rather trivial —
reflexion with which she dies.

The remaining characters of the tragedy are drawn with
varying degrees of force; but they all seem to stand forth
as real human figures under the lurid glare of a storm-laden

sky: nor is it easy to analyse the impression created by
so dense a mixture of unwholesome humours, wild passions,
and fearful sorrows. The total effect is unspeakably
ghastly — though in one of the most elaborately terrible
scenes the intention becomes too obvious, and 'several
forms of distraction' exhibited by the mad Cornelia strike
one as in some degree conventional, as they are to some
extent plagiarised.

It must however be observed that in this play, as in
'The Duchess of Malfi,' Webster creates some of his most
powerful effects by single touches — flashes of genius
which seem to light up of a sudden a wide horizon of
emotions. It is in these flashes, so vivid as to illu-
mine the dullest perception, so subtle as to search the
closest heart, that Webster alone among our dramatists can
be said at times to equal Shakspere.

'The Duchess of Malfi' (first printed in 1623) bears to
my mind the signs of a more matured workmanship than 'The
White Devil.' The action is indeed full of horrors, but
not, so to speak, clogged with them; the tragic effect
is not less deep, but pity may claim an equal share in it
with terror. The story (taken from a novel by Bandello
which through Belleforest's French version found its way
into Paynter's 'Palace of Pleasure') is in itself simple
and symmetrical, and the fifth act (though perhaps rather
excessive in length) seems a natural complement to the
main action. The death of the unhappy Duchess, whose crime
it was to marry her steward from sheer love, is here
avenged upon her brothers and murderers by the instrument
of their own cruelty. In the character of the Duchess
there is little very specially to attract; but she is
drawn with a simplicity not devoid of power, and her art-
lessness is apparently designed to contrast with the dia-
bolical craft of her persecutors. It is not however till
the fourth act that the author has an opportunity of putting forth his peculiar power. He has here accumulated
every element of horror of which the situation seems to
admit (indeed the dance of madmen is in every sense superfluous); the preparations for the Duchess' death are made
in her presence; her coffin is brought in, her dirge is
sung, then she is strangled, to revive only for a moment
in order to learn from her executioner, himself full of
pity and remorse, that her husband still lives. This
act abounds in those marvellous touches of which Webster
is master; the most powerful of them all is the sudden
thrill of pity in the breast of the brother who has commanded her death, on beholding his command fulfilled:

Bos.   Do you not weep?
            Other sins only speak;   murder shrieks out:
            The element of water moistens the earth,
            But blood flies upwards and bedews the heavens.
Ferd.   Cover her face; mine eyes dazzle; she died young.

Although the character of Bosola in this tragedy displays
a composite kind of humour in which the author appears to
have taken a unique kind of pleasure, there is less variety
in the *dramatis personae* as a whole than in those of 'The
White Devil.' But the total impression left upon the mind
by the tragic action of 'The Duchess of Malfi' is unsur-
passed in depth by anything else known to have been
achieved by Webster;   nor is the hope unreasonable that so
masterly a work may permanently recover possession of the
English stage....
        Little needs to be added to the above in the way of
general comment on the characteristics of Webster's dramatic genius.   The wonderful strength of these characteristics displays itself with the utmost distinctness in
'The White Devil' and 'The Duchess of Malfi.'   Webster
loves to accumulate the favourite furniture of theatrical
terror — murders and executions, the dagger and the pistol, the cord and the coffin, together with skulls and
ghosts, and whatever horrors attend or are suggested by
the central horror of them all.   Herein he is not exceptional among the Elisabethans, of whom, from Kyd to Tourneur, so many were alike addicted to the employment of the
whole apparatus of death.   What is distinctive in Webster,
is in the first place the extraordinary intensity of his
imagination in this sphere of ideas, and again the ela-
borateness of his workmanship, which enabled him to surpass — it may fairly be said — all our old dramatists
in a field which a large proportion were at all times
ready to cultivate.   As for later endeavors in our literature to rival this familiarity with death and its ghastly
associations, they have rarely escaped the danger of arti-
ficiality or succeeded in stimulating the imaginative
powers of any generation but their own.   Among all these
poets of the grave and its terrors we meet with but few
whose very soul seems, like Webster's, a denizen of the
gloom by which their creations are overspread.
        But Webster's most powerful plays and scenes are char-
acterised by something besides their effective appeal to
the emotion of terror.   He has a true insight into human
nature, and is capable of exhibiting the operation of
powerful influences upon it with marvellous directness.
He is aware that men and women will lay open the inmost
recesses of their souls in moments of deep or sudden

agitation; he has learnt that on such occasions unexpected contrasts — an impulse of genuine compassion in an
assassin, a movement of true dignity in a harlot — are
wont to offer themselves to the surprised observer; he is
acquainted with the fury and the bitterness, the goad and
the after-sting of passion, and with the broken vocabulary
of grief. All these he knows and understands, and is able
to reproduce, not continually or wearisomely, but with that
unerring recognition of supremely fitting occasions which
is one of the highest, as it is beyond all doubt one of
the rarest, gifts of true dramatic genius.

It is impossible that a dramatist possessing this
faculty should be without humour of a very remarkable
order; and though we unfortunately possess but a single
comedy which can be ascribed to Webster only, no doubt
can exist as to his possession of the gift in question.
Some of the comic characters in 'The White Devil' (Flamineo and Camillo) are effectively drawn; the dry humour
of Bosola's commentaries on life and its vicissitudes in
'The Duchess of Malfi' has a quite original savour; and
if Webster is to be held to have had any share in 'A Cure
for a Cuckold,' I cannot see why it should be thought
self-evident that he was guiltless of any of its unre-
fined, but far from spiritless, fun. His satirical powers
are great, as may be seen from the versatility with which
he varies his attacks upon the favourite subject of his
social satire — the law, its practice and its practitioners.

It was equally out of the question that the characteristic powers of Webster's dramatic genius should have been
unaccompanied by fine poetic feeling. Of this he occasionally gives evidence in passages of considerable beauty,
though upon imagery he appears to have bestowed no very
marked attention. I am not aware that either in the respect of particular passages, or of entire scenes, Webster's
debt to Shakspere is so large as it has been represented
to be; and I must confess my ignorance as to what support
can (with the exception of Cornelia's madness) be found for
Hazlitt's assertion that Webster's two most famous tragedies
are 'too like Shakespear, and often direct imitations of
him, both in general conception and individual expression.'
On the other hand, the same critic seems by no means to go
too far in saying that this author's plays 'upon the whole
perhaps come the nearest to Shakespear of anything we have
on record.' What more requires to be said in acknowledgment
of the true dramatic genius of which Webster was possessed?

But at the same time the meaning of the assertion should
not be pressed beyond certain definite limits. In his
power of revealing dramatically by truthful touches the
secrets of human nature, Webster was like Shakspere. He

was unlike him in but rarely combining with this power the
art of exhibiting dramatically the development of character
under the influence of incident.   The collapse of Bracciano's
strength of will and of Appius' self-control under the influence of passion and of opportunity are forcibly brought
home to us;   but the White Devil herself, as her name is
intended to imply, is an abnormal, though not impossible,
being;   while the Duchess of Malfi can hardly be said to
have a character at all.   What Webster in general repro-
duces with inimitable force, is a succession of situations
of overpowering effect;   in construction he is far from
strong, and in characterisation he only exceptionally
passes beyond the range of ordinary types.   There seems
little moral purpose at work in his most imposing efforts;
and his imagination, instead of dwelling by preference on
the associations of the law-court and the charnel-house,
would have had to sustain itself on nutriment more diverse
and more spiritual, in order to wing his mighty genius to
freer and loftier flights.

36.   SWINBURNE ON WEBSTER

1882, 1886

Algernon Charles Swinburne (1837-1909) was Webster's most
enthusiastic champion in the late nineteenth century, and
his extravagant and impressionistic praise led to fierce
rejoinders from theatrical critics such as Archer and Shaw.
For although Swinburne writes that Webster's fame 'assuredly does not depend upon the merit of a casual passage here
or there', an examination of dramatic structure has little
place in Swinburne's view of Webster as moral poet.   He
stands as the chief spokesman for the line of Victorian
critics who celebrate Webster's poetic imagination and
who place him at Shakespeare's right hand in the creation
of poetry, rather than drama.   The legacy of Lamb continued.
   Extracts from (a) John Webster, 'Sonnets on English
Dramatic Poets' ('The Complete Works of A.C. Swinburne',
ed. Edmund Gosse and T.J. Wise (1925), V, p. 177) and (b)
John Webster, 'The Nineteenth Century', XIX, pp. 861-81.
The essay was slightly revised for his last work, 'The
Age of Shakespeare' (1908).

(a)Thunder: the flesh quails, and the soul bows down.
   Night: east, west, south, and northward, very night.
   Star upon struggling star strives into sight,
   Star after shuddering star the deep storms drown.
   The very throne of night, her very crown,
   A man lays hand on, and usurps her right.
   Song from the highest of heaven's imperious height
   Shoots, as a fire to smite some towering town.
   Rage, anguish, harrowing fear, heart-crazing crime,
   Make monstrous all the murderous face of Time
   Shown in the spheral orbit of a glass
   Revolving. Earth cries out from all her graves.
   Frail, on frail rafts, across wide-wallowing waves,
   Shapes here and there of child and mother pass.

(b) There were many poets in the age of Shakespeare who
make us think, as we read them, that the characters in
their plays could not have spoken more beautifully, more
powerfully, more effectively, under the circumstances
imagined for the occasion of their utterance: there are
only two who make us feel that the words assigned to the
creatures of their genius are the very words they must
have said, the only words they could have said, the actual
words they assuredly did say. Mere literary power, mere
poetic beauty, mere charm of passionate or pathetic fancy,
we find in varying degrees dispersed among them all alike;
but the crowning gift of imagination, the power to make us
realize that thus and not otherwise it was, that thus and
not otherwise it must have been, was given — except by
exceptional fits and starts — to none of the poets of
their time but only to Shakespeare and to Webster.
   Webster, it may be said, was but as it were a limb of
Shakespeare: but that limb, it might be replied, was the
right arm. 'The kingly-crowned head, the vigilant eye,'
whose empire of thought and whose reach of vision no
other man's faculty has ever been found competent to match,
are Shakespeare's alone for ever: but the force of hand,
the fire of heart, the fervour of pity, the sympathy of
passion, not poetic or theatric merely, but actual and
immediate, are qualities in which the lesser poet is not
less certainly or less unmistakably pre-eminent than the
greater. And there is no third to be set beside them: not
even if we turn from their contemporaries to Shelley himself. All that Beatrice says in 'The Cenci' is beautiful
and conceivable and admirable: but unless we except her
exquisite last words — and even they are more beautiful
than inevitable — we shall hardly find what we find in
'King Lear' and 'The White Devil,' 'Othello' and 'The

Duchess of Malfy';   the tone of convincing reality;   the
note, as a critic of our own day might call it, of certi-
tude.
    There are poets — in our own age, as in all past ages —
from whose best work it might be difficult to choose at a
glance some verse sufficient to establish their claim —
great as their claim may be — to be remembered for ever;
and who yet may be worthy of remembrance among all but the
highest. Webster is not one of these: though his fame
assuredly does not depend upon the merit of a casual
passage here or there, it would be easy to select from
any one of his representative plays such examples of the
highest, the purest, the most perfect power, as can be
found only in the works of the greatest among poets.
There is not, as far as my studies have ever extended, a
third English poet to whom these words might rationally
be attributed by the conjecture of a competent reader.

    We cease to grieve, cease to be fortune's slaves,
    Nay, cease to die, by dying.

There is a depth of severe sense in them, a height of
heroic scorn, or a dignity of quiet cynicism, which can
scarcely be paralleled in the bitterest or the fiercest
effusions of John Marston or Cyril Tourneur or Jonathan
Swift. Nay, were they not put into the mouth of a criminal cynic, they would not seem unworthy of Epictetus....
    The first quality which all readers must recognize, and
which may strike a superficial reader as the exclusive or
excessive note of his genius and his work, is of course his
command of terror. Except in Aeschylus, in Dante, and in
Shakespeare, I at least know not where to seek for passages
which in sheer force of tragic and noble horror — to the
vulgar shock of ignoble or brutal horror he never condescends to submit his reader or subdue his inspiration — may
be set against the subtlest, the deepest, the sublimest
passages of Webster. Other gifts he had as great in themselves, as precious and as necessary to the poet: but
on this side he is incomparable and unique. Neither Marlowe nor Shakespeare had so fine, so accurate, so infallible a sense of the delicate line of demarcation which
divides the impressive and the terrible from the horrible
and the loathsome — Victor Hugo and Honoré de Balzac from
Eugène Sue and Emile Zola. In his theatre we find no presentation of old men with their beards torn off and their
eyes gouged out, of young men imprisoned in reeking cess-
pools and impaled with red-hot spits. Again and again his
passionate and daring genius attains the utmost limit and
rounds the final goal of tragedy;   never once does it

break the bounds of pure poetic instinct.   If ever for a
moment it may seem to graze that goal too closely, to
brush too sharply by those bounds, the very next moment
finds it clear of any such risk and remote from any such
temptation as sometimes entrapped or seduced the foremost
of its forerunners in the field.   And yet this is the
field in which its paces are most superbly shown.   No
name among all the names of great poets will recur so soon
as Webster's to the reader who knows what it signifies,
as he reads or repeats the verses in which a greater than
this great poet — a greater than all since Shakespeare —
has expressed the latent mystery of terror which lurks in
all the highest poetry or beauty, and distinguishes it
inexplicably and inevitably from all that is but a little
lower than the highest....
     Few instances of Webster's genius are so well known as
the brief but magnificent passage which follows;   yet it
may not be impertinent to cite it once again.

>   *Brachiano*. O thou soft natural death, that art joint
>   twin
> To sweetest slumber!   no rough-bearded comet
> Stares on thy mild departure; the dull owl
> Beats not against thy casement; the hoarse wolf
> Scents not thy carrion; pity winds thy corpse,
> Whilst horror waits on princes.
>   *Vittoria*. I am lost forever.
>   *B*. How miserable a thing it is to die
> 'Mongst women howling! — What are those?
>   *Flamineo*. Franciscans:
> They have brought the extreme unction.
>   *B*. On pain of death, let no man name death to me;
> It is a word infinitely terrible.

The very tremor of moral and physical abjection from nervous defiance into prostrate fear which seems to pant and
bluster and quail and subside in the natural cadence of
these lines would suffice to prove the greatness of the
artist who could express it with such terrible perfection:
but when we compare it, by collation of the two scenes,
with the deep simplicity of tenderness, the childlike
accuracy of innocent emotion, in the passage previously
cited, it seems to me that we must admit, as an unques-
tionable truth, that in the deepest and highest and purest
qualities of tragic poetry Webster stands nearer to Shakespeare than any other English poets stands to Webster;   and
so much nearer as to be a good second;   while it is at least
questionable whether even Shelley can reasonably be accepted
as a good third.   Not one among the predecessors, contempor-

aries, or successors of Shakespeare and Webster has given
proof of this double faculty — this coequal mastery of
terror and pity, undiscoloured and undistorted, but vivi-
fied and glorified, by the splendour of immediate and infallible imagination. The most grovelling realism could
scarcely be so impudent in stupidity as to pretend an
aim at more perfect presentation of truth: the most fer-
vent fancy, the most sensitive taste, could hardly dream
of a desire for more exquisite expression of natural passion in a form of utterance more naturally exalted and
refined.
     In all the vast and voluminous records of critical
error there can be discovered no falsehood more foolish
or more flagrant than the vulgar tradition which represents this high-souled and gentle-hearted poet as one
morbidly fascinated by a fantastic attraction towards the
'violent delights' of horror and the nervous or sensational excitements of criminal detail; nor can there be
conceived a more perverse or futile misapprehension than
that which represents John Webster as one whose instinct
led him by some obscure and oblique propensity to darken
the darkness of southern crime or vice by an infusion of
northern seriousness, of introspective cynicism and re-
flective intensity in wrongdoing, into the easy levity
and infantile simplicity of spontaneous wickedness which
distinguished the moral and social corruption of renascent
Italy. Proof enough of this has already been adduced to
make any protestation or appeal against such an estimate
as preposterous in its superfluity as the misconception
just mentioned is preposterous in its perversity. The
great if not incomparable power displayed in Webster's
delineation of such criminals as Flamineo and Bosola —
Bonapartes in the bud, Napoleons in a nutshell, Caesars
who have missed their Rubicon and collapse into the likeness of a Catiline — is a sign rather of his noble English
loathing for the traditions associated with such names as
Caesar and Medici and Borgia, Catiline and Iscariot and
Napoleon, than of any sympathetic interest in such incar-
nations of historic crime....
     The fifth act of 'The Duchess of Malfy' has been assailed
on the very ground which it should have been evident to a
thoughtful and capable reader that the writer must have
intended to take up — on the ground that the whole upshot
of the story is dominated by sheer chance, arranged by mere
error, and guided by pure accident. No formal scheme or
religious principle of retribution would have been so
strangely or so thoroughly in deeping with the whole scheme
and principle of the tragedy. After the overwhelming
terrors and the overpowering beauties of that unique and

marvellous fourth act in which the genius of this poet
spreads its fullest and its darkest wing for the longest
and the strongest of its flights, it could not but be
that the subsequent action and passion of the drama should
appear by comparison unimpressive or ineffectual;   but
all the effect or impression possible of attainment under
the inevitable burden of this difficulty is achieved by
natural and simple and straightforward means.   If Webster
has not made the part of Antonio dramatically striking
and attractive — as he probably found it impossible to do —
he has at least bestowed on the fugitive and unconscious
widower of his murdered heroine a pensive and manly grace
of deliberate resignation which is not without pathetic
as well as poetical effect.   In the beautiful and well-
known scene where the echo from his wife's unknown and new-
made grave seems to respond to his meditative mockery and
forewarn him of his impending death, Webster has given such
reality and seriousness to an old commonplace of contemporary fancy or previous fashion in poetry that we are
fain to forget the fantastic side of the conception and
see only the tragic aspect of its meaning.   A weightier
objection than any which can be brought against the conduct of the play might be suggested to the minds of some
readers —   and these, perhaps, not too exacting or too
captious readers —   by the sudden vehemence of transformation which in the great preceding act seems to fall
like fire from heaven upon the two chief criminals who
figure on the stage of murder.   It seems rather a miraculous retribution, a judicial violation of the laws of
nature, than a reasonably credible consequence or evolution of those laws, which strikes Ferdinand with madness and Bosola with repentance.   But the whole atmosphere of the action is so charged with thunder that this
double and simultaneous shock of moral electricity rather
thrills us with admiration and faith than chills us with
repulsion or distrust.   The passionate intensity and moral
ardour of imagination which we feel to vibrate and penetrate through every turn and every phrase of the dialogue
would suffice to enforce upon our belief a more nearly
incredible revolution of nature or revulsion of the soul.
     It is so difficult for even the very greatest poets to
give any vivid force of living interest to a figure of
passive endurance that perhaps the only instance of perfect triumph over this difficulty is to be found in the
character of Desdemona.   Shakespeare alone could have made
her as interesting as Imogen or Cordelia;   though these
have so much to do and dare, and she after her first
appearance has simply to suffer: even Webster could not
give such individual vigour of characteristic life to the

figure of his criminal heroine. Her courage and sweetness,
her delicacy and sincerity, her patience and her passion,
are painted with equal power and tenderness of touch: yet
she hardly stands before us as distinct from others of her
half angelic sisterhood as does the White Devil from the
fellowship of her comrades in perdition.

But it is only with Shakespeare that Webster can ever
be compared in any way to his disadvantage as a tragic
poet: above all others of his country he stands indis-
putably supreme. The place of Marlowe indeed is higher
among our poets by right of his primacy as a founder and
a pioneer: but of course his work has not — as of course
it could not have — that plenitude and perfection of dramatic power in construction and dramatic subtlety in detail which the tragedies of Webster share in so large a
measure with the tragedies of Shakespeare. Marston, the
poet with whom he has most in common, might almost be said
to stand in the same relation to Webster as Webster to
Shakespeare. In single lines and phrases, in a few de-
tached passages and a very few distinguishable scenes,
he is worthy to be compared with the greater poet; he
suddenly rises and dilates to the stature and strength of
a model whom usually he can but follow afar off. Marston,
as a tragic poet, is not quite what Webster would be if his
fame depended simply on such scenes as those in which the
noble mother of Vittoria breaks off her daughter's first
interview with Brachiano — spares, and commends to God's
forgiveness, the son who has murdered his brother before
her eyes — and lastly appears 'in several forms of distraction,' 'grown a very old woman in two hours,' and
singing that most pathetic and imaginative of all funereal
invocations which the finest critic of all time so justly
and so delicately compared to the watery dirge of Ariel.
There is less refinement, less exaltation and perfection
of feeling, less tenderness of emotion and less nobility
of passion, but hardly less force and fervour, in the very
best and loftiest passages of Marston: but his genius is
more uncertain, more fitful and intermittent, less harmonious, coherent, and trustworthy than Webster's. And
Webster, notwithstanding an occasional outbreak into
Aristophanic licence of momentary sarcasm through the
sardonic lips of such a cynical ruffian as Ferdinand or
Flamineo, is without exception the cleanliest, as Marston
is beyond comparison the coarsest writer of his time.

37.   JAMES RUSSELL LOWELL LECTURES

1887

American poet, critic, and diplomat, James Russell Lowell
(1819-1891) lectured on The Old English Dramatists at the
Lowell Institute in Boston, finding Webster, like Victor
Hugo, impressive in spite of himself. Extracts from his
hastily written lecture in volume XI of 'The Works of
James Russell Lowell' (1892), pp. 239-61.

In my first lecture I spoke briefly of the deficiency in
every respect of Form which characterizes nearly all the
dramatic literature of which we are taking a summary survey,
till the example of Shakespeare and the precepts of Ben
Jonson wrought their natural effect. Teleology, or the
argument from means to end, the argument of adaptation,
is not so much in fashion in some spheres of thought and
speculation as it once was, but here it applies admirably.
We have a piece of work, and we know the maker of it. The
next question that we ask ourselves is the very natural
one — how far it shows marks of intelligent design. In
a play we not only expect a succession of scenes, but that
each scene should lead, by a logic more or less stringent,
if not to the next, at any rate to something that is to
follow, and that all should contribute their fraction of
impulse towards the inevitable catastrophe. That is to
say, the structure should be organic, with a necessary
and harmonious connection and relation of parts, and not
merely mechanical, with an arbitrary or haphazard joining
of one part to another. It is in the former sense alone
that any production can be called a work of art.
   And when we apply the word Form in this sense to some
creation of the mind, we imply that there is a life, or,
what is still better, a soul in it. That there is an intimate relation, or, at any rate, a close analogy, between
Form in this its highest attribute and Imagination, is
evident if we remember that the Imagination is the shaping
faculty. This is, indeed, its preeminent function, to
which all others are subsidiary....
   Let us, however, come down to what is within the reach
and under the control of talent and of a natural or acquired dexterity. And such a thing is the plot or arrangement of a play. In this part our older playwrights are
especially unskilled or negligent. They seem perfectly

content if they have a story which they can divide at
proper intervals by acts and scenes, and bring at last to
a satisfactory end by marriage or murder, as the case may
be. A certain variety of characters is necessary, but
the motives that compel and control them are almost never
sufficiently apparent. And this is especially true of the
dramatic motives, as distinguished from the moral. The
personages are brought in to do certain things and perform
certain purposes of the author, but too often there seems
to be no special reason why one of them should do this or
that more than another. The obliging simplicity with
which they walk into traps which everybody can see but
themselves, is sometimes almost delightful in its absurdity....
    These thoughts were suggested to me by the gratuitous
miscellaneousness of plot (if I may so call it) in some
of the plays of John Webster, concerning whose works I am
to say something this evening, a complication made still
more puzzling by the motiveless conduct of many of the
characters. When he invented a plot of his own, as in
his comedy of 'The Devil's Law Case,' the improbabilities
become insuperable, by which I mean that they are such as
not merely the understanding but the imagination cannot
get over.... In estimating material improbability as distinguished from moral, however, we should give our old
dramatists the benefit of the fact that all the world was
a great deal farther away in those days than in ours,
when the electric telegraph puts our button into the grip
of whatever commonplace our planet is capable of producing.
    Moreover, in respect of Webster as of his fellows, we
must, in order to understand them, first naturalize our
minds to *their* world. Chapman makes Byron say to Queen
Elizabeth: —

                                      'These stars,
    Whose influence for this latitude,
    Distilled, and wrought in with this temperate air,
    And this division of the elements,
    Have with your reign brought forth more worthy spirits
    For counsel, valour, height of wit, and art,
    Than any other region of the earth,
    Or were brought forth to all your ancestors.'

And this is apt to be the only view we take of that Golden
Age, as we call it fairly enough in one, and that, perhaps,
the most superficial, sense. But it was in many ways rude
and savage, an age of great crimes and the ever-brooding
suspicion of great crimes. Queen Elizabeth herself was the
daughter of a King as savagely cruel and irresponsible as

the Grand Turk.   It was an age that in Italy could breed
a Cenci, and in France could tolerate the massacre of St.
Bartholomew as a legitimate crime of statecraft.   But
when we consider whether crime be a fit subject for tragedy, we must distinguish.   Merely as crime, it is vulgar,
as are the waxen images of murderers with the very rope
round their necks with which they are hanged.   Crime becomes then really tragic when it merely furnishes the
theme for a profound psychological study of motive and
character.   The weakness of Webster's two greatest plays
lies in this — that crime is presented as a spectacle,
and not as a means of looking into our own hearts and
fathoming our own consciousness.

[Lowell recounts in detail the plot of 'The Devil's Law
Case', noting the improbabilities within the action.]

   'The White Devil, or Vittoria Corombona,' produced in
1612, and 'The Duchess of Malfi,' in 1616, are the two
works by which Webster is remembered.   In these plays
there is almost something like a fascination of crime
and horror.   Our eyes dazzle with them.   The imagination
that conceived them is a ghastly imagination.   Hell is
naked before it.   It is the imagination of nightmare,
but of no vulgar nightmare.   I would rather call it fan-
tasy than imagination, for there is something fantastic
in its creations, and the fantastic is dangerously near
to the grotesque, while the imagination, where it is most
authentic, is most serene.   Even to elicit strong emotion,
it is the still small voice that is most effective;   nor
is Webster unaware of this, as I shall show presently.
Both these plays are full of horrors, yet they do move
pity and terror strongly also.   We feel that we are under
the control of a usurped and illegitimate power, but it
is power.   I remember seeing a picture in some Belgian
church where an angel makes a motion to arrest the hand
of the almighty just as it is stretched forth in the act
of creation.   If the angel foresaw that the world to be
created was to be such a one as Webster conceived, we
can fully understand his impulse.   Through both plays
there is a vapor of fresh blood and a scent of churchyard
mould in the air.   They are what children call *creepy*.
Ghosts are ready at any moment: they seem indeed to have
formed a considerable part of the population in those
days.

[Lowell gives the story of 'The White Devil', and quotes
the scene of Marcello's burial.]

In the trial scene the defiant haughtiness of Vittoria,
entrenched in her illustrious birth, against the taunts
of the Cardinal, making one think of Browning's Ottima
'magnificent in sin,' excites a sympathy which must check
itself if it would not become admiration. She dies with
the same unconquerable spirit, not shaming in death at
least the blood of the Vitelli that ran in her veins. As
to Flamineo, I think it plain that but for Iago he would
never have existed; and it has always interested me to
find in Webster more obvious reminiscences of Shakespeare,
without conscious imitation of him, than in any other
dramatist of the time. Indeed, the style of Shakespeare
cannot be imitated, because it is the expression of his
individual genius. Coleridge tells us that he thought he
was copying it when writing the tragedy of 'Remorse,'
and found, when all was done, that he had reproduced
Massinger instead. Iago seems to me one of Shakespeare's
most extraordinary divinations. He has embodied in him
the corrupt Italian intellect of the Renaissance. Flamineo is a more degraded example of the same type, but
without Iago's motives of hate and revenge. He is a mere
incarnation of selfish sensuality. These two tragedies
of 'Vittoria Corombona' and the 'Duchess of Malfi' are,
I should say, the most vivid pictures of that repulsively
fascinating period, that we have in English. Alfred de
Musset's 'Lorenzaccio' is, however, far more terrible,
because there the horror is moral wholly, and never physical, as too often in Webster.

There is something in Webster that reminds me of Victor
Hugo. There is the same confusion at times of what is big
with what is great, the same fondness for the merely
spectacular, the same insensibility to repulsive details,
the same indifference to the probable or even the natural,
the same leaning toward the grotesque, the same love of
effect at whatever cost; and there is also the same im-
pressiveness of result. Whatever other effect Webster may
produce upon us, he never leaves us indifferent. We may
blame, we may criticize, as much as we will; we may say
that all this ghastliness is only a trick of theatrical
blue-light; we shudder, and admire nevertheless. We may
say he is melodramatic, that his figures are magic lantern
pictures that waver and change shape with the curtain on
which they are thrown: it matters not; he stirs us with
an emotion deeper than any mere artifice could stir.

38. SAINTSBURY'S SURVEY

1887

Perhaps the most influential literary historian and critic
of his time, George Saintsbury (1845-1933), Regius Professor of Rhetoric and English Literature at Edinburgh,
stressed positive personal response by the reader as a
major test of literary greatness. Saintsbury implies
that this reader would be grounded in realism and thus find
Webster the creator of great dramatic flashes, and would
have a preference for 'The White Devil'. Extracts from
'A History of Elizabethan Literature', pp. 274-6, 278-80.

Webster's plays are comparatively well known, and there is
no space here to tell their rather intricate arguments.
It need only be said that the contrast of the two ['The
White Devil' and 'The Duchess of Malfi'] is striking and
unmistakable; and that Webster evidently meant in the one
to indicate the punishment of female vice, in the other to
draw pity and terror by the exhibition of the unprevented
but not unavenged sufferings of female virtue. Certainly
both are excellent subjects, and if the latter seem the
harder, we have Imogen and Bellafront to show, in the most
diverse material, and with the most diverse setting possible, how genius can manage it. With regard to 'The
White Devil,' it has been suggested with some plausibility
that it wants expansion. Certainly the action is rather
crowded, and the recourse to dumb show (which, however,
Webster again permitted himself in 'The Duchess') looks
like a kind of shorthand indication of scenes that might
have been worked out. Even as it is, however, the sequence
of events is intelligible, and the presentation of character is complete. Indeed, if there is any fault to find with
it, it seems to me that Webster has sinned rather by too
much detail than by too little. We could spare several of
the minor characters, though none are perhaps quite so
otiose as Delio, Julio, and others in 'The Duchess of
Malfi.' We feel (or at least I feel) that Vittoria's
villainous brother Flamineo is not as Iago and Aaron and
De Flores are each in his way, a thoroughly live creature.
We ask ourselves (or I ask myself) what is the good of the
repulsive and not in the least effective presentment of the
Moor Zanche. Cardinal Monticelso is incontinent of tongue
and singularly feeble in deed, — for no rational man would,

after describing Vittoria as a kind of pest to mankind,
have condemned her to a punishment which was apparently
little more than residence in a rather disreputable but by
no means constrained boarding-house, and no omnipotent
pope would have let Ludivico loose with a clear inkling of
his murderous designs. But when these criticisms and
others are made, 'The White Devil' remains one of the most
glorious works of the period. Vittoria is perfect throughout; and in the justly-lauded trial scene she has no superior on any stage. Brachiano is a thoroughly life-like portrait of the man who is completely besotted with an evil
woman. Flamineo I have spoken of, and not favourably; yet
in literature, if not in life, he is a triumph; and above
all the absorbing tragic interest of the play, which it is
impossible to take up without finishing, has to be counted
in. But the real charm of 'The White Devil' is the wholly
miraculous poetry in phrases and short passages which it
contains. Vittoria's dream of the yew-tree, almost all
the speeches of the unfortunate Isabella, and most of her
rival's, have this merit. But the most wonderful flashes
of poetry are put in the mouth of the scoundrel Flamineo,
where they have a singular effect. The famous dirge which
Cornelia sings can hardly be spoken of now, except in
Lamb's artfully simple phrase 'I never saw anything like
it,' and the final speeches of Flamineo and his sister de-
serve the same endorsement. Nor is even the proud fare-
well of the Moor Zanche unworthy....
    'The Duchess of Malfi' is to my thinking very inferior —
full of beauties as it is. In the first place, we cannot
sympathise with the duchess, despite her misfortunes, as
we do with the 'White Devil.' She is neither quite a
virtuous woman (for in that case she would not have resort-
ed to so much concealment) nor a frank professor of 'All
for Love.' Antonio, her so-called husband, is an unroman-
tic and even questionable figure. Many of the minor
characters, as already hinted, would be much better away.
Of the two brothers the Cardinal is a cold-blooded and
uninteresting debauchee and murderer, who sacrifices sisters and mistresses without any reasonable excuse. Ferdinand, the other, is no doubt mad enough, but not interestingly mad, and no attempt is made to account in any way
satisfactorily for the delay of his vengeance. By common
consent, even of the greatest admirers of the play, the
fifth act is a kind of gratuitous appendix of horrors
stuck on without art or reason. But the extraordinary
force and beauty of the scene where the duchess is murdered; the touches of poetry, pure and simple, which, as
in 'The White Devil,' are scattered all over the play; the
fantastic accumulation of terrors before the climax; and

the remarkable character of Bosola, — justify the high
place generally assigned to the work. True, Bosola wants
the last touches, the touches which Shakespeare would have
given. He is not wholly conceivable as he is. But as a
'Plain Dealer' gone wrong, a 'Malcontent' (Webster's work
on that play very likely suggested him), turned villain,
a man whom ill-luck and fruitless following of courts have
changed from a cynic to a scoundrel, he is a strangely
original and successful study. The dramatic flashes in
the play would of themselves save it. 'I am Duchess of
Malfi still,' and the other famous one 'Cover her face;
mine eyes dazzle; she died young,' often as they have been
quoted, can only be quoted again. They are of the first
order of their kind, and except the 'already my De Flores!'
of 'The Changeling,' there is nothing in the Elizabethan
drama out of Shakespeare to match them.

39. J.A. SYMONDS ON WEBSTER

1888

In his Mermaid edition of the tragedies of Webster and
Tourneur, J.A. Symonds (1840-93), while appreciative of
the moral Webster's 'firm grasp upon the essential qualities of diseased and guilty human nature', furthers the
idea of Webster's plays as mosaics: 'the outlines of the
Fable, the structure of the drama as a complete work of
art, seem to elude our grasp'. Symonds prefigures Eliot
and others who would agree that Webster's 'general impression' is 'blurred'. Extracts from 'Webster and
Tourneur', pp. xii-xxiii.

It is just this power of blending tenderness and pity with
the exhibition of acute moral anguish by which Webster is
so superior to Tourneur as a dramatist.
    Both playwrights have this point in common, that their
forte lies not in the construction of plots, or in the
creation of characters, so much as in an acute sense for
dramatic situations. Their plots are involved and stippled
in with slender touches; they lack breadth, and do not
rightly hang together. Their characters, though forcibly
conceived, tend to monotony, and move mechanically. But

when it is needful to develop a poignant, a passionate, or
a delicate situation, Tourneur and Webster show themselves
to be masters of their art.   They find inevitable words,
the right utterance, not indeed always for their specific
personages, but for generic humanity, under the *peine forte
et dure* of intense emotional pressure.   Webster, being the
larger, nobler, deeper in his touch on nature, offers a
greater variety of situations which reveal the struggles
of the human soul with sin and fate.   He is also better
able to sustain these situations at a high dramatic pitch —
as in the scene of Vittoria before her judges, and the
scene of the Duchess of Malfi's assassination.   Still Tourneur can display a few such moments by apocalyptic flashes —
notably in the scenes where Vendice deals with his mother
and sister.
     Both playwrights indulge the late Elizabethan predilec-
tion for conceits.   Webster, here as elsewhere, proves
himself the finer artist.   He inserts Vittoria's dream,
Antonio's dialogue with Echo, Bosola's Masque of Madmen,
accidentally and subserviently to action.   Tourneur en-
larges needlessly, but with lurid rhetorical effect, upon
the grisly humoufs suggested by the skull of Vendice's
dead mistress.   Using similar materials, the one asserts
his claim to be called the nobler poet by more steady
observance of the Greek precept 'Nothing overmuch'.   Words
to the same effect might be written about their several
employment of blank verse and prose.   Both follow Shakespeare's distribution of these forms, while both run verse
into prose as Shakespeare never did.   Yet I think we may
detect a subtler discriminative quality in Webster's most
chaotic periods than we can in Tourneur's;   and what upon
this point deserves notice is that Webster, of the two,
alone shows lyrical faculty.   His three dirges are of exquisite melodic rhythm, in a rich low minor key;   much of
his blank verse has the ring of music;   and even his
prose suggests the colour of song by its cadence.   This
cannot be said of the sinister and arid Muse of Tourneur....
[Webster] is not a poet to be dealt with by any summary
method; for he touches the depths of human nature in ways
that need the subtlest analysis for their proper explana-
tion.   I am, however, loth to close without a word or two
concerning the peculiarities of Webster's dramatic style.
Owing to condensation of thought and compression of language, his plays offer considerable difficulties to readers
who approach them for the first time.   So many fantastic
incidents are crowded into a single action, and the dialogue is burdened with so much profoundly studied matter,
that the general impression is apt to be blurred.   We rise
from the perusal of his Italian tragedies with a deep sense

of the poet's power and personality, an ineffaceable
recollection of one or two resplendent scenes, and a clear
conception of the leading characters. Meanwhile the outlines of the fable, the structure of the drama as a complete work of art, seem to elude our grasp. The persons,
who have played their part upon the stage of our imagination, stand apart from one another, like figures in a
tableau vivant. 'Appius and Virginia', indeed, proves
that Webster understood the value of a simple plot, and
that he was able to work one out with conscientious firm-
ness. But in 'Vittoria Corombona' and 'The Duchess of
Malfi', each part is etched with equal effort after luminous effect upon a murky background; and the whole play
is a mosaic of these parts. It lacks the breadth which
comes from concentration on a master-motive. We feel that
the author had a certain depth of tone and intricacy of
design in view, combining sensational effect and sententious pregnancy of diction in works of laboured art. It
is probable that able representation upon the public stage
of an Elizabethan theatre gave them the coherence, the
animation, and the movement which a chamber-student misses.
When familiarity has brought us acquainted with Webster's
way of working, we perceive that he treats terrible and
striking subjects with a concentrated vigour special to
his genius. Each word and trait of character has been
studied for a particular effect. Brief lightning flashes
of astute self-revelation illuminate the midnight darkness
of the lost souls he has painted. Flowers of the purest
and most human pathos, like Giovanni de Medici's dialogue
with his uncle in 'Vittoria Corombona', bloom by the charnel-
house on which the poet's fancy loved to dwell. The culmination of these tragedies, setting like stormy suns in
blood-red clouds, is prepared by gradual approaches and
degrees of horror. No dramatist showed more consummate
ability in heightening terrific effects, in laying bare
the inner mysteries of crime, remorse, and pain combined
to make men miserable. He seems to have had a natural
bias toward the dreadful stuff with which he deals so
powerfully. He was drawn to comprehend and reproduce abnormal elements of spiritual anguish. The materials with
which he builds are sought for in the ruined places of
abandoned lives, in the agonies of madness and despair, in
the sarcasms of reckless atheism, in slow tortures, griefs
beyond endurance, the tempests of sin-haunted conscience,
the spasms of fratricidal bloodshed, the deaths of frantic
hope-deserted criminals. He is often melodramatic in the
means employed to bring these psychological elements of
tragedy home to our imagination. He makes free use of
poisoned engines, daggers, pistols, disguised murderers,

masques, and nightmares. Yet his firm grasp upon the
essential qualities of diseased and guilty human nature,
his profound pity for the innocent who suffer shipwreck
in the storm of evil passions not their own, save him, even
at his gloomiest and wildest, from the unrealities and
extravagances into which less potent artists — Tourneur,
for example — blundered. That the tendency to brood on
what is ghastly belonged to Webster's idiosyncrasy appears
in his use of metaphor. He cannot say the simplest thing
without giving it a sinister turn — as thus:

> you speak as if a man
> Should know what fowl is coffn'd in a bak'd meat,
> Afore you cut it up.
> ('The White Devil', IV ii 19-21)

> When knaves come to preferment, they rise as gallowses
> are raised i'th' Low Countries, one upon another's
> shoulders.
> ('The White Devil', II i 320-22)

> Pleasure of life! what is't? only the good hours
> Of an ague.
> ('The Duchess of Malfi', V iv 67-8)

> I would sooner eat a dead pigeon taken from the soles
> of the feet of one sick of the plague, than kiss one
> of you fasting.
> ('The Duchess of Malfi', II i 38-40)

In his dialogue, people bandy phrases like — '0 you
screech-owl!' and 'Thou foul black cloud!' A sister warns
her brother to think twice before committing suicide, with
this weird admonition:

> I prithee yet remember,
> Millions are now in graves, which at last day
> Like mandrakes shall rise shrieking.
> ('The White Devil', V vi 65-7)

But enough now has been said about these peculiarities
of Webster's dramatic style. It is needful to become
acclimatised to his specific mannerism, both in the way of
working and the tone of thinking before we can appreciate
his real greatness as a dramatic poet and moralist.

40. THE TYPICAL WEBSTER

1892

___

From 'The Nature and Elements of Poetry', p. 249, by E.C.
Stedman (1833-1908), poet, critic, and editor. A highly
esteemed member of the New York literary circle of his
day, Stedman affords us a microcosm of Webster criticism.
The book is comprised of lectures given by Stedman at Johns
Hopkins University in 1891.

___

At the outset of English poetry, Chaucer's imagination is
sane, clear-sighted, wholesome with open-air feeling and
truth to life. Spenser's is the poet's poet chiefly as
an artist. The allegory of 'The Faerie Queene' is not
like that of Dante, forged at white heat, but the symbol-
ism of a courtier and euphuist who felt its unreality.
But all in all, the Elizabethan period displays the English
imagination at full height. Marlowe and Webster, for example, give out fitful but imaginative light which at times
is of kindred splendor with Shakespeare's steadfast beam.
Webster's 'Duchess of Malfi' teaches both the triumphs and
the dangers of the dramatic fury. The construction runs
riot; certain characters are powerfully constructed,
others are wild figments of the brain. It is full of
most fantastic speech and action; yet the tragedy, the
passion, the felicitous language and imagery of various
scenes, are nothing less than Shakesperean. To comprehend
rightly the good and bad qualities of this play is to have
gained a liberal education in poetic criticism.

41. 'THE DUCHESS OF MALFI' IN LONDON

1892

___

On 21 October 1892, the Independent Theatre Society presented 'The Duchess of Malfi', adapted and staged by
William Poel, at the Opera Comique. Poel's version consisted of some scene rearrangements but, unlike Horne's
adaptation, had few additions to Webster's text. Moments

of sensationalism included luminous skeletons painted on
the backs of the madmen. Mary Rorke portrayed the Duchess
with Murray Carson as Bosola, and both 'perhaps regretted
their involvement: the reviews as a whole were not good,
and Webster on the stage again proved a problem. The
Independent Theatre Society, formed in part to preserve
through staging various old masterpieces, would later pro-
mote early performances of Ibsen and Shaw.
    Extracts from (a) the 'Nation', 10 November 1892,
pp. 348-9; (b) 'The Times', London, 22 October 1892,
p. 6; (c) Clement Scott's review in the 'Illustrated
London News', 29 October 1892, p. 539.

(a)   ...Perhaps I might as well say at once how deeply
I regret that the Society is so much more praiseworthy in
intention than in achievement. In the present deplorable
dramatic stagnation, one does not like to find fault where
there is certainly a striving in the right direction. But
unfortunately the effect of a play upon the stage depends
wholly and entirely on the manner in which it is inter-
preted by actors and actresses, and this is doubly true
when the play is a tragedy in verse, dating back to a day
when dramatic ideals were not as ours, and when, in point
of dramatic construction, Shakespere was a giant among
pigmies. I venture to say that it would be absolutely
out of the question to give an unrevised version of the
'Duchess of Malfi,' though this fact does not excuse the
Independent Theatre Society's unexpected squeamishness in
suppressing some of the more vigorous Elizabethan passages.
The changes made, however, were chiefly in the arrangement
of the scenes, and here Mr. William Poel, the Shakespere
scholar, had a work made to his hand. But, despite his
labors, scene followed scene and incident succeeded incident with an irrelevancy and a suddenness that left one
fairly bewildered. The deadly hatred of Duke and Cardinal
for their sister, even before she has married her steward
without their leave, one had to accept simply, without
asking for a reason, as one accepts the screen in the
modern society play, or the convenient arrangement of
doors in the modern farce. The motives of Bosola, the
hired murderer, discoursing of pity, singing the dirge,
as it were, of his own victim, was another problem for
which one did not seek the solution. The intrigue of the
Cardinal with Julia apparently had no other use in the
tragedy save to add one more corpse to the many strewing
the stage in that indescribable fifth act, which even
Webster's most ardent admirers think superfluous. In a

word, to make the play, even after revision, not only
convincing, but possible, to a modern audience, it must
be consummately well rendered by trained and experienced
actors who understand the value of the lines and their
proper delivery. The programme, on the night of the
performance, quoted the critical appreciations of Lamb,
who thought that only a Webster could move a horror skilfully or touch a soul to the quick;   of Mr. Swinburne, who
declared no poet to be morally nobler than Webster;   of
Mr. Symonds, who finds his excellence in his power of
blending tenderness and pity with the exhibition of acute
moral anguish;   of Mr. Gosse, who ranks the 'Duchess of
Malfi' as second only to 'King Lear.' But to read a
drama in the library is a very different thing from seeing
it performed on the stage. If the beauty and power depend
upon the lines rather than the construction, then, when
those lines are cruelly murdered in the mouths of second-
rate or inexperienced actors, beauty and power disappear
and tragedy degenerates into burlesque.

Miss Mary Rorke, who played the Duchess, is an actress
of some refinement and dignity in mediocre parts, but her
entire misconception of what was expected of her was shown
by her close study of Miss Ellen Terry's methods. It were
a charity not to give the name of the man who parodied the
Duke, and ranted and raved up and down the stage, so that
from the very first, instead of waiting until the end of
the fourth act, Bosola might have proclaimed him distraught.
But to me it was Bosola (Mr. Murray Carson) who was the
chief offender, because of his greater pretensions. He
began at that high pitch where the wise tragedian leaves
off;   he spoke with his eyes, his nostrils, his forehead;
he writhed and grimaced so unrestrainedly that by the end
of the first act he had exhausted his resources, and could
but begin and go through the same tricks all over again.
As for the others, the kindest that can be said is that
their incapacity was a trifle less aggressive — probably
because their roles were more than a trifle less important.
Lowell was also quoted on the playbill. 'Whatever effect,'
he says, 'Webster may produce upon us, he never leaves us
indifferent.' At moments when the audience should have
wept they tittered, and this, too, in the fourth act, where
horror crowds upon horror in the long ingenious torture
to which the Duchess is submitted as a preparation for her
own murder. However, it was in this same act that the one
scene adequately impressive was presented;   an impressive-
ness due not a little to the fact that not a word was
spoken, while 'ladies' in Holbein dress danced the Dance
of Death with grinning skeletons, to the far tap, tap of
a muffled drum, and the Duchess, in her white robes, sat

watching, reading herdoom in every step, her faithful
Cariola crouched at her knees.
    Mr. Green and his society proposed to give aspiring
actors and actresses the chance, elsewhere denied, of a
hearing in parts suited to them — an admirable proposi-
tion. But to aid and abet the incompetent in the full
display of their incompetency is another matter. It is
just here that the directors of the Independent Theatre
so far have followed such a mistaken policy. They may yet
discover rare talent in new playwrights, they may revive
old masterpieces; but until for the interpretation of
their dramatists they find actors and actresses of fair
average ability and intelligence, their performances, art-
istically, must be failures. Who would want to listen to
Wagner ground out of a hurdy-gurdy? Who would want to
look at a Titian on the canvas of the cheap copyist? I,
for my part, would rather never have seen Webster's 'Duchess of Malfi' on the stage than to have allowed the sad
parody presented on the boards of the Opera Comique on
Friday last.

(b) In its quest of the extravagant and the horrifying,
the Independent Theatre has chanced upon 'The Duchess of
Malfi,' of which it gave a special performance last night
at the Opera Comique. It is not clear with what object
this revival is undertaken by Mr. Green's society. Webster's tragedy has fallen upon evil days. It is no stranger
to the stage, since it is occasionally played in suburban
and provincial theatres, like dramas of the 'Sweeney Todd'
and 'The Castle Spectre' type, for the sake of its horrors.
The acting versions of the piece are, of course, more or
less mutilated; but the Independent Theatre, which plays
a version arranged by Mr. W. Poel, does not show any particular reverence for the poet's text, and, indeed, from a
prefatory note to the first edition, which professes to
contain 'diverse things that the length of the play would
not bear in the presentment,' it would appear that the
tragedy never has been acted as printed. Most of the
adapters have introduced into the old play matter of their
own, this being the case even with the version played by
Phelps at Sadler's Wells 40 years ago; and Mr. Poel, if
he has not altered anything on his own account, has at
least borrowed from other sources, the Duchess, for example,
being strangled, not on the stage, but in the wings,
whither she is borne for that purpose, as in Theobald's
version. A greater liberty still now taken with the
classic is the introduction of a so-called 'Dance of Death,'
an effect well-known, we believe, in the music halls,

whereby a group of dancers, thanks to a costume trick,
suddenly assume the semblance of skeletons. On the other
hand, the gruesome scenes with the madmen are greatly
shorn of their original proportions and the dance of madmen omitted. The play, as now performed, can only be
considered attractive by reason of its nightmarelike
scenes enacted in the prison, where the Duchess is put
to death. Slowly and deliberately performed on what, for
the most part, is a darkened stage, its long drawn-out
intrigue would be found oppressive and tiresome by an
ordinary audience. Miss Mary Rorke claims a certain
amount of sympathy for the hapless Duchess, and Mr. Murray
Carson as Bosola, the instrument of the murder, has some
thrilling and impressive moments. Ferdinand and the Cardinal, who plan their sister's assassination because of
her secret marriage with Antonio, are embodied by Mr.
Barraclough and Mr. James Roe. If the play were put up
for a run, further excisions of the text would be advis-
able, three hours and a half of its horrors, native and
imported, being a too liberal allowance.

(c) The earnest and enthusiastic members of the Independent Theatre Society have given us a very interesting
and complete performance of old Webster's fine tragedy,
'The Duchess of Malfi'. This glorious play, so far as
literature is concerned, has been approached in a very
reverential spirit, and it was put on the stage with
extreme care; and, on the whole, this most difficult work
was very creditably acted by the young people engaged.
The Duchess of Miss Mary Rorke, though uninspired, was a
pathetic and poetically graceful performance.... But head
and shoulders above all the rest was the Bosola of Mr.
Murray Carson. He was like a bit of old Sadler's Wells,
and it is a pity that one who has such a fine stage face,
such a rich and ringing voice, and such an admirable elo-
cutionary method should have been born in an age that dis-
cards not only tragedy but the whole range of poetic
drama.... And oh! what a treat to the tortured ear to hear
good poetry declaimed like this, without a trace of bombast
in it, but with just emphasis, nice balance, and true feeling! It was a musical as well as a dramatic treat.

42.   ARCHER ATTACKS

1893

William Archer (1856-1924), drama critic, playwright, and
translator of Ibsen, was a central force in promoting the
new drama of Ibsen and Shaw. For Archer, a vitriolic
attack on earlier drama was one method of making way for
public acceptance of the new. Totally grounded in the
'well-made play' of rational construction and realistic
effect, Archer, though misguided and incorrigibly uninformed about Elizabethan dramatic conventions, cannot be
wholly patronized: as Robert Ornstein has noted, 'his
attacks on the formlessness of Webster's plays contained
an irreducible kernel of aesthetic truth' ('The Moral
Vision of Jacobean Tragedy' (1960), p. 128).
      Archer's first barrage in January 1893 appeared as
Webster, Lamb, and Swinburne, following the William Poel
production of 'The Duchess' in 1892; from the 'New
Review', VIII, pp. 96-106. He would later review a 1919
ill-fated production at Hammersmith of 'The Duchess' in
'Nineteenth Century', LXXXXVII (January 1920), pp. 126-32,
and publish it in a revised and expanded version in his
pThe Old Drama and the New' (1924). This was the production in which Ferdinand died standing on his head, and it
was all Archer needed.

The recent performance of Webster's 'The Duchess of Malfi'
at the Independent Theatre must have done one good service
if no other. It must have brought home to many of the
audience the need for a careful scrutiny of what may be
called the Lamb tradition with respect to the Elizabethan
dramatists. To say so is to take your life in your hands,
for never had critical tradition devouter or more puissant
champions. I myself, in making the suggestion, am conscious of a feeling of impiety. To the most fanatical
worshipper of Charles Lamb I would say, 'Nay, an thou'lt
mouth I'll rant as well as thou', were it not that the
motion with which one thinks of that exquisite spirit is
so intimate and personal as to seem almost profane by
utterance. In the love of Lamb, I take it, all literary
sects and parties are at one. Not to love him is to place
yourself without the pale of literature, almost of humanity.
Nor do I for a moment deny that the discovery, the illumination, the revivifying of the Elizabethan drama is one of

his chief claims upon our gratitude. In the dark treasure-
cave where jewels and dross had long lain indistinguishable,
he said, 'Let there be light', and there was light. The
gems shone forth, a possession for ever: and if the discoverer's eyes were a little bit dazzled, if he now and
then mistook the superficial glitter of the dross for the
inborn glow of the jewel, shall that be held to detract
from the value and the renown of his discovery? It is,
after all, his humanity that we love in Lamb: and humanity
is not infallible.

I see, on second thoughts, that I have used a misleading
image. My point is not that Lamb mistook dross for jewels,
but that he now and then mistook the value of the dramatic
setting in which he found his poetic jewels enchased. He
regarded the Elizabethan drama too much in the light of
absolute literature, making it a law unto itself. He
took too little account of the historic influences, the
material conditions, under which it was produced; and in
this the inheritors and expounders of his doctrine have
faithfully followed his lead. Poetry — pure beauty, force,
dignity, perfection of utterance — is in reality one and
eternal. What is well said is well said, whether it be
addressed to Ionian villagers or to Roman courtiers, to the
populace of sixteenth-century London, or to the exquisites
of seventeenth-century Versailles. And that which seems
well said because of its consonance with a temporary fashion, is in reality ill said. Fine style is fine style —
and poetry is the fine flower of fine style — in virtue
of its harmony with primal instincts, with universal laws
of perception and association, with fundamental conditions
of intellectual, emotional, and sensuous life. It appeals
to no conventions, to no ephemeral modes of thought; wherefore it may be studied and appraised as a thing in itself,
apart from all historical or sociological knowledge. Drama,
on the other hand, is a thing of convention, of fashion.
The drama of any given period (in so far as it is a natural, not a merely imitative, product) is strictly a part
of its manners and customs, and must be studied as a social
institution. Its merits and defects must be read in the
light of the material and intellectual circumstances which
gave it birth, and the conventions of one period must not
be mistaken for everlasting canons of art. Lamb and his
disciples, as it seems to me, are subject to this illusion.
Their knowledge of the Elizabethan period is imperfect on
the historical side, and on the literary side so intimate
as to be uncritical. Is this a paradox? Surely not. Is
it not rather a truism that if we stand too near a given
object we cannot see it in its true relations and proportions? Lamb read himself into the literature of the period

until he himself became an Elizabethan in spirit. His
moral and aesthetic perceptions, and especially his
notions of dramatic effect, became wholly Elizabethan-
ized. 'Elia hath not so fixed his nativity', he declared
in one of his most whimsical papers, 'but that, if he
seeth occasion, he will be born again in whatever place,
and at whatever period, shall seem good unto him.' By
way of preparation for his study of the Elizabethans he
seems to throw back his nativity from 1775 to 1575. This
makes his criticism delightful, but inconclusive. Prince
Posterity must not abdicate the privileges, which are
also the duties, of his heirship to the ages. In dealing with an art so absolutely conditioned by time and
place as the drama, we must not sublimate into an ideal
·and practice, even the noblest practice, of one particular
period, and that, so far as its theatrical audiences were
concerned, a semi barbarous one. By all means let us be
capable, on occasion, of taking the Elizabethan point of
view; but let us not therefore abandon for ever the point
of view of universal art, or, in other words, of right
reason. Lamb's estimate of the pure poetry contained in
the Elizabethan drama will always be valid, for excellence
of style, as aforesaid, is one and eternal. Whoso has
eyes to see it at all is always at the right point of
view. But in drama, even under what may be called the
poetical convention, pure beauty of expression is a subordinate and inessential quality; and Lamb, I submit, was
not at the right point of view for estimating the Elizabethan drama as drama, in its relation to other dramatic
literatures and to the ideal of dramatic creation. His
disciples, too, partly by reason of their discipleship,
have failed to place themselves at the just point of view.
They have, if anything, exaggerated his tendency to make
the Elizabethan drama a law unto itself. Therefore, I
repeat, it is high time that the whole Lamb tradition
should be subjected to careful scrutiny.
    I have neither the learning, the leisure, nor the skill
for such a task. For the present, at any rate, I can
only attempt, in a few desultory remarks on 'The Duchess
of Malfi', to indicate to better qualified critics the
line of thought which, as it seems to me, they ought to
follow. Onlookers, we know, see most of the game, and an
outsider may sometimes attain to a clearer and saner
vision of things than is possible for an adept. Special-
ist criticism, if I may call it so, has in Mr. Swinburne
an illustrious and redoubtable champion. In learning,
insight, sympathy, eloquence, he stands alone. Were
I to measure myself against him in all or any of these
qualities, my presumption would be such as it would tax

even his rhetoric to characterize. My will, like Orlando's,
hath in it a more modest working. Far from presuming to
rival him as an expert, I claim no advantage save that of
inexpertness, detachment of mind, comparative aloofness of
standpoint. Erudition will not always guide a critic to
the best point of view. Intensity of vision may even be
deceptive if the object be not approached at the proper
angle.

Let me in the first place clear the ground, and refresh
the reader's memory, by means of a brief synopsis of 'The
Duchess of Malfi'. Webster found in Bandello the bare
incident of a marriage between a Duchess of Malfi and her
major-domo, both of whom are killed at the instigation of
her brother, the Cardinal of Arragon. Bandello casually
mentions 'Bosolo' as the name of the man who shot Antonio;
and there is also a vague reference to an unnamed brother
of the Cardinal's. To all intents and purposes, however,
the play, both as regards character and incident, is of
Webster's own invention. He borrowed scarcely a single
detail from the Italian novel.

In the first act, at Malfi, Ferdinand, Duke of Calabria,
and his brother, the Cardinal of Arragon, in parting from
their sister, the widowed Duchess of Malfi, warn her, in
threatening terms, not to think of marrying again. They
set one Bosola to spy upon her actions. No sooner are
their backs turned than the Duchess summons her major-domo,
Antonio Bologna, proposes marriage to him, and marries him
(per verba [de] presenti, as she puts it) on the spot. In
the second act, Bosola suspects that the Duchess is pregnant, and lays a trap to make her reveal her condition.
This hastens her delivery, and Bosola's suspicion is converted into certainty when he picks up a paper in which
Antonio has cast the nativity of the new-born child. It
never occurs to him that Antonio may be the father; but he
posts off to Rome to inform his employers of his discovery.
Bosola's intelligence annoys the Cardinal, and throws
Ferdinand into a foul-mouthed frenzy of rage, which brings
the act to a close. Ferdinand's frenzy, however, is not
a furor brevis. He is so patient in his wrath that before
the third act opens, his sister, living in undisturbed
conjugal felicity, has had two more children. Bosola is
still spying upon her and eager to discover her paramour,
but does not even now suspect Antonio. Ferdinand, by means
of a secret door, enters his sister's chamber and upbraids
her savagely, professing as his motive an extreme concern
for her lost virtue. Seeing that they are on the brink of
discovery, she accuses Antonio of embezzlement and pretends
to dismiss him from her service, promising to follow him to
Ancona, where he is to take refuge. Bosola, by affecting

sympathy with the disgraced Antonio, worms her secret out
of her, and of course makes known the truth to his employers. The action now wanders to Loretto, where Antonio
and the Duchess are separated. Antonio takes refuge in
Milan, and the Duchess, captured by Bosola, is led back to
Malfi.

We now come to what Mr. Swinburne calls 'the overwhelming terrors and the overpowering beauties of that unique
and marvellous fourth act, in which the genius of this
poet spreads its fullest and its darkest wing for the longest and the strongest of its flights'. The scene is the
room in her palace in which the Duchess is imprisoned.
Ferdinand, entering the dark, pretends to be reconciled
with her, and gives her, instead of his own hand, that of
a dead man, leading her to believe that it is Antonio's.
Then a curtain is drawn back, and (in an alcove, I suppose) are revealed waxen images representing the dead
bodies of Antonio and their children. The Duchess does
not suspect the trick which is being played upon her, and
(oddly enough) makes no attempt to approach or touch the
supposed corpses. A grief-stricken woman might be expected
to kiss her dead children, and so discover the fraud; but
the Duchess is too much taken up (as Lamb puts it) with
'speaking the dialect of despair', and saying things that
have 'a snatch of Tartarus and the sould in bale', to
think of any such simple and natural proceeding. Then
Ferdinand releases the mad-folk from 'the common hospital',
and sets them 'to sing and dance and act their gambols to
the full o' the moon' around her chamber. Presently they
enter, singing:

> O, let us howl, some heavy note,
>   Some deadly dogged howl,
> Sounding as from the threat'ning throat
>   Of beasts, and fatal fowl!
>
> > (IV ii 61-4)

They indulge in ribald ravings, dance a dance 'with
music answerable thereto', and then go off again as Bosola
enters, disguised as an old man. He announces himself as
a tomb-maker, introduces 'executioners, with a coffin,
cords, and a bell', and proceeds to speak 'the living person's dirge' in order 'to bring her by degrees to mortification'. Then the Duchess is strangled, her children are
strangled, and her maid, Cariola, is strangled, all on
the open stage. Ferdinand goes mad at sight of this
slaughter-house, and Bosola, suddenly penitent, sets off
for Milan to carry the news to Antonio. In the fifth act,
at Milan, the Cardinal's mistress, Julia, is poisoned;

Bosola kills Antonio, mistaking him for the Cardinal; then
he kills the Cardinal's servant, the Cardinal himself, and
Ferdinand, who, by the way, is still raving mad; and Ferdinand, before he dies, kills Bosola. Antonio's friend,
Delio, and one of the children are left alive.
In this tragedy, then, five men, three women, and two
children come to violent ends, the children and two of the
women being strangled on the open stage; yet, says Mr.
Swinburne,

> in all the vast and voluminous records of critical
> error there can be discovered no falsehood more foolish
> or more flagrant than the vulgar tradition which repre-
> sents this high-souled and gentle-hearted poet as one
> morbidly fascinated by a fantastic attraction towards
> the 'violent delights' of horror, and the nervous or
> sensational excitements of criminal detail.
>   'What', [says Lamb] 'are "Luke's iron crown", the bra-
> zen bull of Perillus, Procrustes' bed, to the waxen
> images which counterfeit death, to the wild masque of
> madmen, the tomb-maker, the bell-man, the living per-
> son's dirge, the mortification by degrees! To move a
> horror skilfully, to touch a soul to the quick, to lay
> upon fear as much as it can bear, to wean and weary a
> life till it is ready to drop, and then step in with
> mortal instruments to take its last forfeit; this
> only a Webster can do. Writers of an inferior genius
> may "upon horror's head horrors accumulate", but they
> cannot do this. They mistake quantity for quality, they
> "terrify babes with painted devils", but they know not
> how a soul is capable of being moved; their terrors
> want dignity, their affrightments are without decorum.'

Well, well! We are to understand, then, that the hideous
and dragged-in antics of insanity constitute a decorous
affrightment, and that the public strangling of two little
children is not a 'violent delight'!
When we thus find great critics putting forth judgements
which read like extravagant and wanton paradoxes, must we
not suspect an illusion somewhere? Their expressions are,
on the face of it, in flagrant contradiction with the
facts (which the reader may verify for himself) set forth
in my account of the play. But from such an account,
from a bald narrative of facts, what element is necessar-
ily excluded? Clearly that of style, of verbal felicity,
of what Mr. Swinburne calls 'literary power, poetic beauty,
charm of passionate or pathetic fancy'. Now in these qualities — qualities of which Lamb and Mr. Swinburne are
judges beyond all appeal — Webster undoubtedly stands

very high.   In spite of a metrical laxity which Mr. Swinburne himself deplores, this play contains many passages
of great inherent beauty, and a still greater number of
speeches of a quaint and, so to speak, unexpected dramatic
force and appropriateness.   Take for instance Antonio's
speech when the Duchess feigns to dismiss him from her
household:

> O, the inconstant
> And rotten ground of service! — you may see
> 'Tis ev'n like him, that in a winter night
> Takes a long slumber o'er a dying fire,
> As loth to part from't; yet parts thence as cold
> As when he first sat down.
>
> (III ii 198-203)

Here, again, is an often-quoted speech of the Duchess to
Cariola while the madmen are howling round her apartment:

> I'll tell thee a miracle —
> I am not mad yet, to my cause of sorrow.
> Th' heaven o'er my head seems made of molten brass,
> The earth of flaming sulphur, yet I am not mad:
> I am acquainted with sad misery,
> As the tann'd galley-slave is with his oar;
> Necessity makes me suffer constantly,
> And custom makes it easy...
>
> (IV ii 23-30)

I could fill page after page with passages of the like
imaginative beauty and vitality, but must content myself
with reminding the reader of the immortal dirge, and quoting these four lines from it:

> Of what is't fools make such vain keeping?
> Sin their conception, their birth weeping;
> Their life a general mist of error,
> Their death a hideous storm of terror.
>
> (IV ii 186-9)

The man who wrote this was in truth a poet, and Mr. Swinburne may, if he is so disposed, class him as 'a lesser
poet only than the greatest'.   It must be remembered, indeed, that he was one of 'the early risers of literature'
who 'found language with the dew upon it' — in other
words, he lived at a period when comparatively small men
had the knack of writing astonishingly great verse.   But
that is a side consideration, and nothing to the present
purpose.   What is certain is that the writings of Webster

are full of 'literary power, poetic beauty, and charm of
passionate and pathetic fancy'. Is it not possible that
these qualities, to which they are so keenly sensitive may
have misled Lamb and Mr. Swinburne? Receiving great delight from a work in dramatic form, may they not have concluded too hastily that their pleasure was due to its
dramatic merits, and transferred to the characters and the
fable admiration which belongs by right to the language and
the imagery? In a word, may they not have mistaken a low
form of drama for a high, and even the highest, because
they found it robed in regal purple of pure poetry?

Whatever may have been Webster's personal tastes, there
cannot be the smallest doubt that the average Elizabethan
audience was avid of 'the "violent delights" or horror,
and the nervous or sensational excitements of criminal
detail'. It is futile to pretend that either the gallants
and masked fair ones in the 'rooms', or the citizens and
'prentices in the 'yard' did not love bloodshed and physical horror in action, reckless crudity, and even deliberate
lewdness, in speech. No playwright of the period failed
to minister to these tastes, for in Elizabeth's time, no
less than in our own, the drama's laws the drama's patrons
gave. The stage was not only the vehicle for the highest
poetry and philosophy of the time; it was also its Punch
and its Pick-Me-Up, its London Journal, its Police News
and its Penny Dreadful. In respect of physical horror,
at any rate, Shakespeare pandered less to the mob than
almost any of his contemporaries, and in nothing did he
show more clearly that he was not of an age but for all
the time. Nor can we doubt that several even of the
choicest spirits of the age, found the less difficulty in
gratifying the popular taste for gruesomeness and gore,
because their own imagination was haunted in a strange un-
canny fashion by the legendary crimes of the Italian Renaissance. Was not this pre-eminently the case of Webster?
When we find a playwright, in his two acknowledged masterpieces, drenching the stage with blood even beyond the
wont of his contemporaries and searching out every possible
circumstance of horror — ghosts, maniacs, severed limbs
and all the paraphernalia of the charnel-house and the
tomb — with no conceivable purpose except just to make our
flesh creep, may we not reasonably, or rather must we not
inevitably, conclude that he either revelled in 'violent
delights' for their own sake, or wantonly pandered to the
popular craving for them? If Mr. Swinburne accepts the
latter alternative — if he would have us believe that the
Webster of the tragedies is not the real Webster, but is
playing an abhorrent part to ingratiate himself with the
groundlings — then his position, if essentially unprovable,

is also essentially incontrovertible. But I do not understand him to claim any private or peculiar knowledge of
Webster's character. What he evidently means is that in
these very tragedies we can discover the 'high soul' and
'gentle heart' of the poet, and can not discover any morbid predilection for 'violent delights'. High-souled and
gentle-hearted he may possibly have been, for these qualities are not incompatible with the vilest perversions of
the aesthetic sense. But to argue that Webster's aesthetic
sense was refined and unperverted is simply to maintain
that black is white and blood is rose-water.

'Webster does not deal in horrors for their own sake',
we shall be told, 'but uses them as means towards the
illustration and development of character'. Could he not
have made clear to us the resignation and fortitude of the
Duchess of Malfi without the ghastly mummery of the dead
hand and the waxen corpses? To argue so is simply to deny
his competence as a dramatic poet. I have heard it main-
tained that the strangling of Cariola is designed to contrast with that of the Duchess — the frantic terror of
the maid serving to throw into relief the noble courage
of the mistress. Who can fail to perceive that if this
were the intention, the death of the maid must of necessity precede that of the mistress, not follow it, as in
Webster? When an effect of contrast is aimed at, and the
things to be contrasted cannot be displayed simultaneously,
it is clear that the minor, so to speak, must precede the
major, the darkness must precede the light. In other
words, the background must be established before the object to be set off against it is presented to our view.
And then the children! What effect of contrast is served
by the massacre of the innocents? Whose character does it
serve to illustrate? Their mother is already dead, or at
least unconscious. Had they been strangled before her
eyes, the effect would have been one of unparalleled , in-
tolerable brutality, but it would, in a certain sense, have
been dramatic. As it is, their death is a mere mechanical
piling of horror upon horror. It does not even throw
any new light on the character of Bosola; when a man is
wading in blood, an inch more or less is no great matter.
What it does throw light upon is the character, or at
least the aesthetic sense, of Webster and his public. It
is perfectly evident that Elizabethan audiences found a
pleasurable excitement in the crude fact of seeing little
children strangled on the stage, and that Webster, to say
the least of it, had no insuperable objection to gratifying that taste.

     Far be it from me to argue that horror has not its legi-
timate place in literature and in drama. 'To move a horror

skilfully, to touch a soul to the quick' is neither an
easy nor an unworthy task. My point is that in 'The
Duchess of Malfi' (and, to a minor degree, in 'The White
Devil') the horrors are unskilfully moved — that they
are frigid, mechanical, brutal. Literature is literature
in virtue of the brain-power implicit in it; and there
goes no more brain power to the invention of these massacres
and monstrosities than to carving a turnip lantern and stick-
ing it on a pole.

Much might be said, if space permitted, of Webster's
construction and characterization. Of dramatic concentration he did not dream. Though a younger man than Shakespeare (whose 'right happy and copius industry' he bracketed
with that of Dekker and Heywood, and postponed to the loftier talents of Chapman and Jonson), he reverted to a stage
of literary development which Shakespeare had outgrown. In
'The White Devil' and 'The Duchess of Malfi' the differen-
tiation between romance and drama is still incomplete. They
are not constructed plays, but loose-strung, go-as-you-
please romances in dialogue. The motivation of 'The Duchess of Malfi' is haphazard even beyond the Elizabethan
average. No motive is assigned in the earlier part of the
play for the brother's virulent and almost monomaniac oppo-
sition to the very idea of their sister's marrying again.
After her death, Ferdinand explains that he hoped to gain
'an infinite mass of treasure' if she died unmarried, and
we may presume that the Cardinal would have been his co-
heir. But this motive, even when we are tardily informed
of it, does not account for his epilepsies of rage and
cruelty, which seem sometimes to spring from regard for
the family honour, sometimes from a rabid enthusiasm for
'virtue' in the abstract. Perhaps we are to understand
that all these motives combine to work up his fundament-
ally cruel nature to the pitch of madness. This might be
a plausible theory enough, but we arrive at it only by
conjecture. It is more than doubtful whether Webster
himself was at all clear as to his characters' motives.
In Ferdinand he provided Burbage with an effective part in
which to 'tear a cat', and neither author, actor, nor
audience inquired too curiously into the reasons for his
frenzies and his cruelties. A similar difficulty confronts
us in Bosola. This 'moody and mocking man of blood' is
certainly not, like the ordinary melodramatic villain,
hewn all of one piece. There is an appearance of subtlety
in his character because it is full of contradictions. But
there is no difficulty in making a character inconsistent;
the task of the artist is to show an underlying harmony
between the apparently conflicting attributes. Bosola
seems sometimes to revel in his infamy, at others to be

the unwilling instrument of a power he cannot resist. 'And
though I loathed the evil,' he says to Ferdinand after the
massacre, 'yet I loved you that did counsel it.' But this
is the first and last we hear of any sentimental devotion
on the spy's part towards his employers; nor can we discover the smallest ground for such a feeling. Mr. Swinburne himself has a momentary misgiving as to 'the sudden
vehemence of transformation, which seems to fall like fire
from Heaven upon the two chief criminals who figure on the
stage of murder'. But he quickly pulls himself together,
explaining that 'the whole atmosphere of the action is so
charged with thunder that this double and simultaneous
shock of moral electricity rather thrills us with admiration and faith than chills us with repulsion and distrust'.
On the whole, I am inclined to think that Webster came very
near to creating in Bosola one of the most complex and most
human villains in drama, a living illustration of that age-
old but ever new paradox: 'Video meliora, proboque;
deteriora sequor.' But the fatal lack of clearness ruins
everything. We cannot help feeling from time to time that
the poet is writing for mere momentary effect, and has
suffered the general scheme of the character to slip out
of sight. All we can say with confidence is that, artis-
tically, Bosola is worth a score of Flamineos. The way
in which the action is suffered to straggle over quite unnecessary stretches of time and space bespeaks the romance
rather than the drama. Ferdinand's fury becomes doubly
incredible and ineffective when two years or more are suffered to elapse between his reception of Bosola's intelligence and his descent upon the Duchess. The only advantage of this delay is that but for it we should have to go
without the massacre of the innocents. The relevance of
the passage in which Delio makes love to the Cardinal's
mistress utterly escapes me; indeed Julia is altogether a
mere excrescence on the play. In shifting the scene to
Loretto, Webster seems at first sight to have slavishly and
mechanically followed Bandello; but his motive was probably to work in the dumb-show pageant of the Cardinal's
military investiture. This to-ing and fro-ing, in any
case, seriously enfeebles the action. The right, if need
be, to jump not only from Amalfi to Ancona, but from China
to Peru, is certainly one of the vital privileges of the
romantic drama; but it is no less certain that changes of
scene must be justified by some clear artistic advantage,
else they merely injure the general effect. Wantonly to
ignore the unities is no less an error than to sacrifice
everything to their observance.
    This is scarcely the place in which to consider Mr.
Swinburne's assertion that 'Webster is without exception

the cleanliest writer of his time'. I think it must be
based on some private interpretation of the term 'cleanly';
but I do not profess to have weighed grossness against
grossness with any nicety. The point, at any rate, is
quite inessential. The gist of my argument, so far as it
can be summed up in a phrase, is this: that Webster was
not, in the special sense of the word, a great dramatist,
but was a great poet who wrote haphazard dramatic or melodramatic romances for an eagerly receptive but semi-barbar-
ous public.

43. WILLIAM POEL DEFENDS WEBSTER

1893

William Poel (1852-1934), actor, theatre manager, and pro-
ducer, founded the Elizabethan Stage Society (1894-1905)
in an important effort to produce the earlier dramatists
under Elizabethan staging conditions. He produced 'The
Duchess' in October 1892, and generated Archer's first attack. From A New Criticism of Webster's 'The Duchess of
Malfi', 'Library Review', II (1893), pp. 21-4.

In a recent number of the 'New Review' Mr. Archer expresses
the opinion that Webster was 'a great poet who wrote haphazard dramatic romances for an eagerly receptive but semi-
barbarous public'; and adds that Webster excels in verbal
felicity, and in writing beautiful language which is full
of imagery and literary power. Of Webster's dramatic felicity and dramatic power Mr. Archer is apparently incredu-
lous. The play of 'The Duchess of Malfi' is 'robed in
regal purple of pure poetry', but the dramatic setting in
which the poetic jewels are enchased is valueless. In
other words, Webster's verse to be admired must be disso-
ciated from the play for which it is written. But Webster's
poetry, of all others, cannot be separated from its dramatic
interest. The immortal dirge may be, as Mr. Archer affirms,
true poetry, but coming from the lips of Bosola at a moment
when the suffering woman is facing her own grave, the words
have an additional force and meaning. They become then
convincing. Nor is it reasonable to ignore the dramatic
instinct needed to conceive dialogue that gives point to

the situation. Later on in the same scene Bosola says to
Ferdinand

> You have bloodily approv'd the ancient truth,
> That kindred commonly do worse agree
> Than remote strangers.
>
> (IV ii 270-2)

and these words, in themselves pregnant with knowledge of
human nature, are made doubly suggestive by the dramatist's
skill in having them spoken at the moment when the action
gives reality to them. In fact, Webster's most celebrated
passages are not great simply because they are pre-eminent
in beauty of idea and felicity of expression, but because
they carry with them dramatic force by being appropriate to
character and situation. 'The real object of the drama,'
says Macaulay, 'is the exhibition of human character, and
those situations which most signally develop character form
the best plot.' Judged by this standard, a well-construc-
ted play may be trifling, dull, and unnatural, while 'a
haphazard dramatic romance' that has in it some scenes
inferior in power and passion to nothing in the whole
range of the drama, may entitle the author to the position
of a great dramatist.

A difficulty in appreciating the actions and motives of
Webster's characters may arise from that imperfect historical knowledge which we are told is the characteristic
of Lamb's criticism. Webster wrote his play not for the
purpose of dealing 'in horror for horror's sake', nor
'just to make the flesh creep', but with a desire to give
vital embodiment to the manners and morals of the Italian
Renaissance, as they appeared to the imagination of Englishmen. As Vernon Lee ably points out, it was the very strangeness and horror of Italian life, as compared with the dull
decorum of English households, that constituted the attraction of Italian tragedy for Elizabethan playgoers. They
were familiar with the saying that 'nothing in Italy was
cheaper than human life'. Their own Ascham had written
that he found in Italy, during a nine days' stay in one
small city, more liberty to sin 'than ever he heard tell
of in our noble citie of London in nine yeare'. No wonder,
then, if the metaphysical judgement of the Puritan urged
Elizabethan dramatists to show, by the action of their
dramas, that there existed a higher power than the mere
strength of those fiercer passions which occurred in Italy,
the land of passion in the sixteenth century. Looked at
from this point of view, much in the play that is unintel-
ligible can be explained. Burckhardt, in his 'Renaissance
of Italy', tells us that a warm imagination kept ever alive

the memory of injuries, real or supposed; more especially
in a country that allowed each man to take the law into
his own hands. Not only a husband, but even a brother, in
order to satisfy the family honour, would take upon himself the act of vengeance; nor would a father scruple to
kill his own daughter, if the dignity of his house had
been compromised by an unworthy marriage. Besides, an
Italian's revenge was never a half-and-half affair. The
Duchess's children are 'massacred' because the whole name
and race of Antonio must be rooted out. Cariola, too,
must die, because she helped to bring about the hated marriage. It is this desire for truth to Italian life that
causes Webster to introduce Julia, and the pre-eminently
Italian dialogue between Julia and Delio. Without Julia
we do not get our typical Cardinal of the Italian Renaissance, a man experienced in simony, poisoning, and lust.
There is even a higher motive for her appearance in the
play. She is designed as a set-off to the Duchess; as
an instance of unholy love in contrast to the chaste love
of the Duchess. Bosola is a masterly study of the Italian
'familiar', who is at the same time a humanist. He is
refined, subtle, indifferent, cynical. A criminal in
action but not in constitution. A man forced by his
position to know all the inward resources of his own
nature, passing or permanent, and conscious of the possibility of a very brief period of power and influence. It
is necessary, moreover, in judging of this play to take
into consideration the restrictions put upon the dramatist
by the novelist. Webster's audience was too familiar with
the various incidents of the story to allow of the dramatist ignoring them. In one instance only does Webster
depart from a statement of Bandello, and that is in making
the Cardinal the younger and not the elder brother — an
unaccountable oversight on the part of Bandello — for
Italian Cardinals were invariably the younger sons of
noble houses.
  Mr. Robert Louis Stevenson says that to read a play is
a knack: the fruit of much knowledge, and some imagination, comparable to that of reading score, 'the reader is
apt to miss the proper point of view'. To see dramatic
propriety and dramatic power in 'The Duchess of Malfi',
there may be needed both critical and historical imagination.

44. A TRADITIONALIST PROTESTS

1893

William Watson (1858-1935), poet and critic, fought a
rearguard action for the Victorians against such fin de
siècle figures as Wilde and Beardsley. A champion of the
traditionalist cause in poetry, and defender, as one reviewer wrote, of 'orthodoxy, patriotism, England, home and
duty', Watson, unsurprisingly, was not at home in Webster's world. From 'Excursions in Criticism', pp. 1-22.

...with the present century came a race of critics who
announced with much originality and power that the most
potent spirits of the old drama were not Jonson with his
laborious art, nor Massinger with his surefooted style,
nor Beaumont and Fletcher with their decorative fancy and
lyrical grace, but Marlowe of the 'mighty line,' and Webster of the sombre imagination, and Dekker and Middleton
and Tourneur and Ford.

The most exquisitely gifted of these critics, Charles
Lamb, was fired with all the zeal of a discoverer. In
many instances he absurdly exaggerated the fertility and
beauty of his new-found land, but much must be pardoned to
the pioneer. With adventurers who first look down into
an unmapped world from a 'peak in Darien,' the immediate
impulse is to gaze and marvel rather than accurately observe. To Lamb and Hazlitt the work of the forgotten
dramatists was a region of indescribable glamour and en-
chantment; and no wonder, for of them and their immediate
associates we may say that

They were the first that ever burst
Into that silent sea.

And some of their verdicts are not likely to be annulled
or much modified. Marlowe is a case in point. As the real
founder, though not precisely the initiator, both of English tragedy and English blank verse — as being thus in a
certain sense the father of our poetry more truly than
even Chaucer, for Chaucer's direct influence upon Shakespeare and Milton is not great, while Marlowe's unquestion-
ably is — the immense importance of his position can
scarcely be overstated....

Let us be grateful to that group of ardent explorers
who brushed the thick dust of two centuries from the pages
of our first great dramatic poet; but having tendered
them our gratitude for real and brilliant service performed, we may still consider ourselves at liberty to inquire whether that absence of all just sense of proportion
which distinguishes a contemporary school of criticism —
a school whose loudest, most voluble apostles are capable
of naming Villon in the same breath with Dante — is not
lineally traceable to the imperfect equipoise of zeal and
discretion which could permit Lamb to speak of Ford, for
instance, as belonging to 'the first order of Poets.'...
Reverting to Hazlitt, one is sorry to find that great
critic's sobriety of judgment, as evinced by his coolly
judicial estimate of Ford, deserting him somewhat in the
presence of Webster, of whom he observes: 'His "White
Devil" and "Duchess of Malfi" upon the whole perhaps come
the nearest to Shakespeare of anything we have on record.'
It may be worth while briefly to consider the propriety
of the criticism which brackets the name of John Webster
with the greatest name in literature.
Coming in the immediate wake of the great master, Webster had, of course — as was inevitable with a man of his
epoch — studied under Shakespeare, so to speak, and though
he cannot be said to have 'caught his great language,' yet
something like an echo of the master's utterance may be
heard at times in the pupil's speech. Even this however,
is apt to be delusive, being really in part ascribable to
that general community of tone and likeness of vocabulary
amongst the Elizabethan dramatists, whereby, in a measure,
all the contemporaries of Shakespeare seem to deliver themselves with somewhat of his accent and air. Then, too,
Webster abounds with direct verbal reminiscences of Shakespeare. Plagiarisms I suppose they may be called, but, in
truth, they are but petty larcenies of a kind having no
deep dye of turpitude. Dryden says of Ben Jonson, refer-
ring to his spoliations of the classics, 'there is scarce
a poet or historian among the Roman authors of those times
whom he has not translated in "Sejannus" and "Catiline."
But he has done his robberies so openly that we may see he
fears not to be taxed by any law. He invades authors like
a monarch, and what would be theft in other poets is only
victory in him.' This imperial mode of appropriation is
not, however, Webster's manner. In fact, his numerous
little filchings from Shakespeare are of the sneaking
sort; less like heroical spoils of conquest than furtive
nibblings at the vast stores of an inexhaustible granary.
But, in conjunction with broader evidences of style, they
help to show the extent of Shakespeare's literary influence

upon Webster. It was a literary influence almost solely,
a moral influence hardly at all. Shakespeare could teach
something of dramatic art to his immediate successors,
but his large and lucid vision of life was an incommuni-
cable private prerogative. Their habitual attitude of
mind in presence of the deeper issues of existence bears
no essential resemblance to his. Shakespeare now and
again, as in 'Measure for Measure,' resigned himself to a
temporary sojourn in some desert tract of thought or feeling. But cynicism, disgust, and despair, were brief and
casual refuges of his spirit. These moods are the permanent and congenial dwelling-places of minds like Webster's.
In the presence of Shakespeare we feel ourselves in com-
munication with an inexhaustible reservoir of vitality.
Life passes into us from every pore of his mind. We turn
to Webster and it is like exchanging the breath of morn for
the exhalations of the charnel. An unwholesome chill goes
out from him. An odour of decay oppresses the tenebrous
air. This poet's morbid imagination affects us like that
touch of the dead man's hand in one of the hideous scenes
of his own most famous play.

That play is 'The Duchess of Malfi.' Its heroine, the
Duchess, a young widow, has recently married her steward
Antonio. Her powerful brothers, Duke Ferdinand and the
Cardinal, through the agency of their spy and bravo, Bosola,
become aware of her *mesalliance*, and, enraged at the discovery, proceed to put in motion an elaborately infernal
machinery of punishment. She is incarcerated in her palace.
Duke Ferdinand visits her in a darkened chamber and extends
to her at parting a dead man's hand in lieu of his own.
Horrified, she calls for lights, which, being brought, dis-
close the effigies of her husband and children, appearing
as if murdered, and devised so ingeniously,

> By Vincentio Lauriola,
> The curious master in that quality,

as to deceive her with the semblance of nature. From this
point onwards the horrors are dispensed with profuse liberality. Duke Ferdinand, apparently solicitous above all
things that his sister should not suffer *ennui* in her dur-
ance, entertains her with a company of madmen purposely
released from Bedlam. One of them sings a rousing catch,
beginning cheerfully thus: —

> 'O let us howl some heavy note,
> Some deadly dogged howl.'

They dance, — the performance, according to the stage-
direction, being accompanied 'with music answerable there-
unto.' The Bedlamites having retired, Bosola enters.
Bosola is a kind of human gangrene infecting the whole
body of the play. His putrid fancy is ingeniously loathsome, and leaves a trace of slime upon all objects which
it traverses: though it may here be remarked parenthe-
tically that Webster exhibits in general a singular fondness for illustrations drawn from disease and corruption.
In the circuit of his imagery the most frequent halting-
places are the mad-house, the lazar-house, the charnel-
house. But, as was observed, Bosola enters to the Duchess,
announcing that he has come to make her tomb. Afterwards
executioners appear, 'with a coffin, cords, and a bell.'
Finally the Duchess, her woman Cariola, and her children
are strangled on the stage. The play, however, still
drags its festering length through another act, in the
course of which several more or less unpleasant persons
are suitably 'removed,' until the reader, satiated with
such gruesome fare, is left to digest, if he can, his
ghoulish banquet.
    And these gross melodramatic horrors, irredeemable by
any touch of saving imagination — these are the poetic
elements which Lamb, admiring in them what he calls 'their
remoteness from the conceptions of ordinary vengeance,'
seriously, and with all the curious brilliance of his
style, discusses as if such things really belonged to the
domain of pure and noble art. Remote from ordinary conceptions these may be, but remote by any essential superiority of elevation they assuredly are not. Horrors that
are stale and commonplace are, of course, recognized at
once for the cheap and vulgar stuff that they are;   but
horrors that are strange and bizarre do not of necessity
belong to any intrinsically higher level of art;   both are
properly of the same class, inasmuch as they propose to
themselves the excitation of the same order of emotions.
And the truth is, with regard to Webster and his group,
that these men had no sober vision of things. Theirs is
a world that reels in a 'disastrous twilight' of lust and
blood. We rise from Shakespeare enlarged and illumined.
Webster is felt as a contracting and blurring influence.
Like his own Duchess of Malfi, when she exclaims:

    'The heavens o'er my head seem made of molten brass,'

we are oppressed as by a sense of a world which is but a
narrow and noisome prison-house, with the heavens for its
ignoble cope. The pity and terror here are not such as
purify. Life seems a chance medley, a rendezvous of

bewildered phantoms; virtue in this disordered world is
merely wasted, honour bears not issue, nobleness dies unto
itself. What one wishes to protest against is the false
criticism which would elevate him and his group to the
rank of the masters who feed man's spirit, just as we
should protest against the putting forward of a similar
claim in behalf of such a writer, for instance, as Edgar
Poe. Poe was a literary artist of much power; the brilliancy of outline which are not the shadow and light of
nature, yet have their peculiar fascination; but the
authentic masters, are they not masters in virtue of their
power of nobly elucidating the difficult world, not of
exhibiting it in a fantastic lime-light? And after all,
the highest beauty in art is, perhaps, a transcendent propriety. The touches which allure us by strangeness, or
which 'surprise by a fine excess,' belong at best to the
second order of greatness. The highest, rarest, and most
marvellous of all are those which simply compel us to feel
that they are supremely fit and right.
     One has to admit that Webster's fatalism, debased though
it be, — a fatalism expressing itself in such words as
those of Bosola,

     'We are merely the stars' tennis balls, struck and bandied
     Which way please them —'

is in its way impressive; but how unlike the fatalism of
Greek tragedy, from which a certain tonic and astringent
philosophy of life may be extracted! Webster's is merely
a fatalism having its root in a conception of existence as
essentially anarchic. In reading him we lose for the time
all sensation of an ordered governance of things. Life
seems a treacherous phantasm or lawless dream, in which
human shapes chase one another like fortuitous shadows
across an insubstantial arena. The ethical infertility
of such a presentation of the world is manifest enough,
but how shortsighted and shallow the criticism which professes to see any kinship between Shakespeare and a type
of mind so defective in sanity of vision, so poor in
humour, so remote from healthful nature, so out of touch
with genial reality! 'A gulf or estuary of the sea which
is Shakespeare!' The image is picturesque but unveracious,
conveying as it does a suggestion of open sunlight and
bracing briny air which is utterly foreign to Webster's
talent. His art is no breezy inlet of any ocean, but
rather a subterranean chamber where the breath and light
of morning never penetrate. In the palace of life he seems
to inhabit, by preference, some mouldy dungeon, peopled
with spectral memories, and odorous of death.

And herein is shown the vast distance of such men from
Shakespeare. The airy amplitudes, the azure spaces of
his mind, are apparent to everyone. The others stifle you
with murderous walls. And it is, perhaps, not altogether
fanciful to surmise that this very characteristic of their
art may have had something to do with the secret of its
special fascination for Charles Lamb. External nature, it
is notorious, had no hold upon him; that exquisite genius
was anything but at home under the open sky. The world as
seen by a picturesque torchlight rather than by candid sunlight attracted his gaze. And it was a torchlighted world,
a world of alternate deep shadow and vivid glare, of
Rembrandtesque chiaroscuro, that he found in the minor
Elizabethan drama....
     Enough, however, has been said. Let us take leave of
Shakespeare's dramatic contemporaries and immediate successors with a hearty recognition of one great though ex-
trinsic merit common to them all. They are not gulfs or
estuaries of his ocean, but they stand towards him in one
very serviceable relation, they are his finest imaginable
foils. If we live under the shadow of the Andes, a time
comes when their immensity ceases to be a perpetual aston-
ishment to us. But if Skiddaw and Helvellyn could suddenly be placed in the foreground, we should experience a
renewed sensation of the vastness of Chimborazo and
Aconcagua. If any reader is so unfortunate as to find
that a prolonged familiarity with Shakespeare begets at
last a some what blunted sensibility to the master's
supreme power, a remedy is at hand by which his palate
may recover its gust. Let him try a course of Webster
and Dekker, Randolph and Tourneur, Middleton and Heywood
and Ford.

45. GOSSE ON WEBSTER'S 'TRAGIC POEM'

1894

Extract from 'The Jacobean Poets' by Edmund Gosse (1849-
1928), poet and man of letters. As the first English translator of Ibsen ('Hedda Gabler', 1891), Gosse not surprisingly faults Webster as dramatist, but, unlike his colleague
William Archer, he can praise Webster, as usual, for the
poetry.

Webster's masterpiece is 'The Duchess of Malfy,' of which
it may confidently be alleged that it is the finest tragedy in the English language outside the works of Shakespeare. The poet found his story in that storehouse of
plots, the 'Novelle' of Bandello, but it had been told in
English by others before him. It was one pre-eminently
suited to inflame the sombre and enthusiastic imagination
of Webster, and to inspire this great, irregular and sublime poem. Dramatic, in the accepted sense, it may
scarcely be called. In the nice conduct of a reasonable
and interesting plot to a satisfactory conclusion, Webster is not the equal of Fletcher or of Massinger; some
still smaller writers may be considered to surpass him on
this particular ground. But he aimed at something more,
or at least, something other, than the mere entertainment
of the groundlings. With unusual solemnity he dedicates
his tragedy to his patron as a 'poem,' and his contemporaries perceived that this was a stronger and more
elaborate piece of dramatic architecture than the eye
was accustomed to see built for half a dozen nights, and
then disappear. Ford, when he read 'The Duchess of Malfy,'
exclaimed —

> Crown him a poet, whom nor Rome nor Greece
> Transcend in all theirs for a masterpiece,

and Middleton described it as Webster's own monument,
fashioned by himself in marble. He had the reputation of
being a slow and punctilious writer, among a set of poets,
with whom a ready pen was more commonly in fashion. We
look to Webster for work designed at leisure, and executed
with critical and scrupulous attention. This carefulness,
however, was unfavourable to a well-balanced composition,
the movement of the whole being sacrificed to an extraordinary brilliancy in detailed passages, and though 'The
Duchess of Malfy' has again and again been attempted on
the modern stage, each experiment has but emphasized the
fact that it is pre-eminently a tragic poem to be enjoyed
in the study.
     It is curious that in a writer so distinguished by care
in the working out of detail, we should find so lax a
metrical system as marks 'The Duchess of Malfy.' Here,
again, Webster seems to be content to leave the general
surface dull, while burnishing his own favourite passages
to a high lustre. He has lavished the beauties both of
his imagination and of his verse on what Mr. Swinburne
eloquently calls 'the overwhelming terrors and the overpowering beauties of that unique and marvellous fourth
act, in which the genius of the poet spreads its fullest

and darkest wing for the longest and the strongest of its
flights.'
    This is what Bosola ejaculates when the Duchess dies —

    O, she's gone again! There the cords of life broke.
    O sacred innocence, that sweetly sleeps
    On turtle's feathers, whilst a guilty conscience
    Is a black register wherein is writ
    All our good deeds and bad, a perspective
    That shows us hell! that we can not be suffer'd
    To do good when we have a mind to it!
    This is manly sorrow;
    These tears, I am very certain, never grew
    In my mother's milk: my estate is sunk
    Below the degree of fear: where were
    These penitent fountains while she was living?
    O, they were frozen up! Here is a sight
    As direful to my soul as is the sword
    Unto a wretch hath slain his father. Come,
    I'll bear thee hence,
    And execute thy last will; that's deliver
    Thy body to the reverent dispose
    Of some good women; that the cruel tyrant
    Shall not deny me. Then I'll post to Milan,
    Where somewhat I will speedily enact
    Worth my dejection.

    The characterization of the Duchess, with her inde-
pendence, her integrity, and her noble and yet sprightly
dignity, gradually gaining refinement as the joy of life is
crushed out of her, is one calculated to inspire pity to a
degree very rare indeed in any tragical poetry. The figure
of Antonio, the subject whom she secretly raises to a mor-
ganatic alliance with her, is simply and wholesomely drawn.
All is original, all touching and moving, while the spirit
of beauty, that rare and intangible element, throws its
charm like a tinge of rose-colour over all that might
otherwise seem to a modern reader harsh or crude.
    On one point, however, with great diffidence, the pre-
sent writer must confess that he cannot agree with those
great authorities, Lamb and Mr. Swinburne, who have assert-
ed, in their admiration for Webster, that he was always
skilful in the introduction of horror. In his own mind,
as a poet, Webster doubtless was aware of the procession
of a majestic and solemn spectacle, but when he endeavours
to present that conception on the boards of the theatre,
his 'terrors want dignity, his affrightments want decorum.'
The horrible dumb shows of 'The Duchess of Malfy' — the
strangled children, the chorus of maniacs, the murder of

Cariola, as she bites and scratches, the scuffling and
stabbing in the fifth act, are, it appears to me — with
all deference to the eminent critics, who have applauded
them — blots on what is notwithstanding a truly noble
poem, and what, with more reserve in this respect, would
have been one of the first tragedies of the world.

Similar characteristics present themselves to us in
'The White Devil,' but in a much rougher form. The sketch-
iness of this play, which is not divided into acts and
scenes, and progresses with unaccountable gaps in the
story, and perfunctory makeshifts of dumb show, has been
the wonder of critics. But Webster was particularly interested in his own work as a romantic rather than a theatrical poet, and it must be remembered that after a long
apprenticeship in collaboration, 'The White Devil' was
his first independent play. It reads as though the writer
had put in only what interested him, and had left the rest
for a coadjutor, who did not happen to present himself, to
fill up. The central figure of Vittoria, the subtle,
masterful, and exquisite she-devil, is filled up very
minutely and vividly in the otherwise hastily painted
canvas; and in the trial-scene, which is perhaps the most
perfectly sustained which Webster has left us, we are so
much captivated by the beauty and ingenuity of the murder-
ess that, as Lamb says in a famous passage, we are ready
to expect that 'all the court will rise and make proffer
to defend her in spite of the utmost conviction of her
guilt.' The fascination of Vittoria, like an exquisite
poisonous perfume, pervades the play, and Brachiano
strikes a note, which is the central one of the romance,
when he says to her —

> Thou hast led me like a heathen sacrifice,
> With music and with fatal yokes of flowers,
> To my eternal ruin.

'The White Devil' is not less full than the 'Duchess
of Malfy' of short lines and phrases full of a surprising
melody. In the fabrication of these jewels, Webster is
surpassed only by Shakespeare....

The abrupt withdrawal of Webster from writing for the
stage — a step which he seems to have taken when he was
little over thirty years of age — points to a sense of
want of harmony between his genius and the theatre. In
fact, none of the leading dramatists of our great period
seems to have so little native instinct for stage-craft
as Webster, and it is natural to suppose that in another
age, and in other conditions, he would have directed his
noble gifts of romantic poetry to other provinces of the

art. If it were not absolutely certain that he flourished
between 1602 and 1612, we should be inclined to place the
period of his activity at least ten years earlier. Although in fact an exact contemporary of Beaumont and
Fletcher, and evidently much Shakespeare's junior, a place
between Marlowe and those dramatists seems appropriate to
him, so primitive is his theatrical art, so ingenuous and
inexperienced his notion of the stage. That he preferred
the more stilted and buskined utterances of drama to grace
and suppleness may be gathered from Webster's own critical
distinctions; he has no words of admiration too high for
Chapman and Jonson; Shakespeare he commends, with a touch
of patronage, on a level with Dekker and Heywood, for his
'right happy and copious industry,' placing the romantic
Beaumont and Fletcher above him. This points to a somewhat academic temper of mind, and to a tendency to look
rather at the splendid raiment of drama than at the pro-
ficiency and variety of those who wear it. Webster is an
impressive rather than a dexterous playwright; but as a
romantic poet of passion he takes a position in the very
first rank of his contemporaries.

46. WEBSTER IN THE 'DNB'

1899

Sidney Lee (1859-1926), editor of the 'Dictionary of
National Biography' and biographer of Shakespeare, affords
us the official view of Webster at the end of the century;
the entry still stands in subsequent editions. Though
free from the panegyrics of Swinburne and others, we are
given a Webster whose blank verse is 'more regular than
Fletcher's'. From volume XX, pp. 1031-6.

Although Nathan Drake and some other eighteenth-century
critics had detected in Webster 'a more than earthly
wildness,' it was Charles Lamb who first recognised his
surpassing genius as a writer of tragedy. Subsequently
Hazlitt, and at a later period Mr. Swinburne, bore powerful
testimony to Lamb's justness of view. Webster is obviously
a disciple of Shakespeare, and of all his contemporaries
Webster approaches Shakespeare nearest in tragic power.

But his power is infinitely circumscribed when it is compared with Shakespeare's. His knowledge of his master's
work, too, is sometimes visible in a form suggestive of
plagiarism. His masterpieces are liable to the charge that
they present the story indecisively and at times fail in
dramatic point and perspicuity. Many scenes too strongly
resemble dialogues from romances to render them effective
on the stage. Webster lacked Shakespeare's sureness of touch
in developing character, and his studies of human nature
often suffer from over-elaboration. With a persistence that
seems unjustifiable in a great artist, Webster, moreover,
concentrated his chief energies on repulsive themes and
characters; he trafficked with an obstinate monotony in
fantastic crimes. Nevertheless, he had a true artistic
sense. He worked slowly, and viewed with abhorrence careless
or undigested work. 'No action,' he wrote in the preface to
'The Devil's Law Case,' 'can ever be gracious where the de-
cency of the language and ingenious structure of the scene
arrive not to make up a perfect harmony.' It is proof of
his high poetic spirit that he was capable of illuminating
scenes of the most repellent wrong-doing with miraculous
touches of poetic beauty such as only Shakespeare could
rival. Furthermore, Webster, despite all the vice round
which his plots revolve, is rarely coarse. In depicting the
perversities of passion he never deviated into pruriency,
and handled situations of contentional delicacy with dignified reticence. Webster's dialogue (he seldom essayed soli-
loquy) abounds in rapid imagery. His blank verse is vigorous
and musical. In its general movement it resembles that of
Shakespeare's later plays. It is far less regular than
Marlowe's, but somewhat more regular than Fletcher's. At its
best his language has something of the 'happy valiancy' which
Coleridge detected in Shakespeare's 'Antony and Cleopatra;'
it has consequently no small share of the obscurity which
characterizes Shakespeare's later work. This feature in
Webster impressed his contemporaries, one of whom, Henry
Fitzjeffrey, applied to him the epithet 'crabbed,' and declared that he wrote 'with his mouth awry.' But, as another
contemporary, Middleton, suggested with surer insight, the
force of Webster's tragic genius, despite the occasional in-
distinctness of his utterance and defects of execution, allows no doubt of the essential greatness of his dramatic
conceptions.
    The fame of Webster has spread to France and Germany.
The 'Duchess of Malfy' and 'The White Devil' were published
with an appreciative preface in French translation by Ernest
Lafond in Paris in 1865, and Frederick Bodenstedt devoted
the first volume of his 'William Shakespeare's Zeitgenossen
und ihre Werke' (Berlin, 1858) to a German rendering of extracts from all Webster's plays.

Select Bibliography

This short select bibliography is of works which consider
earlier criticism of John Webster.

HUNTER, G.K. and S.K., 'John Webster, A Critical Anthology'
(1969): critical excerpts from past and present.
MAHANEY, WILLIAM E., 'John Webster: A Classified Bibliography' (1973).
MOORE, DON D., 'John Webster and His Critics, 1617-1964'
(1966): a history of varying major responses to Webster
in the study and on the stage for three centuries.
TANNENBAUM, SAMUEL A., 'John Webster, A Concise Bibliography' (1941).
WANG, TSO-LIANG, 'The Literary Reputation of John Webster
to 1830' (1975): an in-depth account of the earliest reactions to the writer and his tenuous survival in play
lists and dramatic histories.

Index

The index is divided into three parts: I Authors of critical comment; II Webster: life and opinions; summary comment on achievement, style, themes; individual plays; III General Index.

I AUTHORS OF CRITICAL COMMENT

II   JOHN WEBSTER

III   GENERAL INDEX